Music Technology Panic Narratives Beyond Piracy

Music Technology Panic Narratives Beyond Piracy

From Taping to Napster to TikTok

David Arditi

ANTHEM PRESS

Anthem Press
An imprint of Wimbledon Publishing Company
www.anthempress.com

This edition first published in UK and USA 2026
by ANTHEM PRESS
75–76 Blackfriars Road, London SE1 8HA, UK
or PO Box 9779, London SW19 7ZG, UK
and
244 Madison Ave #116, New York, NY 10016, USA

Copyright © 2026 David Arditi

The author asserts the moral right to be identified as the author of this work.

All rights reserved. Without limiting the rights under copyright reserved above, no part of this publication may be reproduced, stored or introduced into a retrieval system, or transmitted, in any form or by any means (electronic, mechanical, photocopying, recording or otherwise), without the prior written permission of both the copyright owner and the above publisher of this book.

British Library Cataloguing-in-Publication Data
A catalogue record for this book is available from the British Library.

Library of Congress Cataloging-in-Publication Data: 2025947341
A catalog record for this book has been requested.

ISBN-13: 978-1-83999-594-1 (Pbk)
ISBN-10: 1-83999-594-7 (Pbk)

This title is also available as an eBook.

CONTENTS

List of Figures   vii

Acknowledgments   ix

1. Introduction: You're Killing Music   1
2. Tape Cassettes and Blank CDs: Home Taping Is Killing Music   13
3. Napster: File-Sharing is Killing Music   25
4. Streaming: User-Generated Video Is Killing Music   39
5. Conclusion: Record Labels Killed Music   55

Bibliography   65

Index   77

LIST OF FIGURES

Figure 2.1.	Global Record Shipments for LPs, Tapes, and CDs	17
Figure 3.1.	CD Sales versus Shipments in the United States (1995–2008)	35
Figure 3.2.	Global Single Sales	37

ACKNOWLEDGMENTS

Every book is the product of a community. When I write about music, I am often thinking about the many musicians I played with in the past. This time, I would like to thank Cameron McLaughlin and George Theka. We played in a dozen different bands together when I was still playing drums, but most importantly as Ethnic Detour, an instrumental jam band. As I wrote, I found myself listening to a live recording we made at an outdoor festival deep in the Jefferson National Forest. Thank you, Cameron and George for helping me think about music.

This also would not have been possible without the support of my colleagues in the Department of Sociology and Anthropology at the University of Texas at Arlington. Thank you, Heather Jacobson, Amy Speier, Jason Shelton, Beth Anne Shelton, Christian Zlolniski, Kelly Bergstrand, Alma Garza, Robert Kunovich, Krystal Beamon, Ritu Khanduri, Naomi Cleghorn, Kelsey Hanson, Robert Young, and Shelley Smith. A special thank you to Robert Bing for his support and guidance at UTA and as a friend who has helped me navigate academia.

My family Debbie Arditi, Bob Arditi, and Amy Kuzemka for instilling my love for music. Jennifer Miller for being a constant sounding board. And Owen Arditi for teaching me what consuming music means in the 2020s.

Chapter 1

INTRODUCTION: YOU'RE KILLING MUSIC

Recorded music runs counter to the history of music performance. Before Thomas Edison and Emile Berliner created the phonograph and gramophone with their respective research and development teams, music only happened "live." The term live itself emerged from the supposed deadness of recorded music. When Edison and Berliner began promoting their inventions, they envisioned recordings as a way to keep the sound of voices after death—the way photographs keep the image of people.[1] Hence the famous Victrola *His Master's Voice* advertising campaign of a dog looking into a phonograph, surprised to hear "his master's voice," who was dead.[2] People even played the "dead" voices at funerals above the casket of the deceased.[3] More profoundly, recorded music allowed people to listen to music on their own.[4] Before the phonograph, it took at least two people to listen to music: one to perform and one to listen. Listening to music was first and foremost a social activity, and it continues to be.[5] While the act of listening becomes individualized, recorded music is built on extended networks of performance, production, distribution, and corporatization. What is key to remember is that even though recorded music is mediated by technology, these processes create the social terrain of recorded music.

With the advent of recorded music, the sociality of music becomes alienated. Alienation occurs when people are separated from other people either physically, socially, or psychologically. Under capitalism, alienation is the separation of workers from the product of their work (i.e., commodities),

---

1 Siefert, "Aesthetics, Technology, and the Capitalization of Culture: How the Talking Machine Became a Musical Instrument."
2 Edge et al., *The Collectors Guide to "His Master's Voice" Nipper Souvenirs.*
3 Edge et al., *The Collectors Guide to "His Master's Voice" Nipper Souvenirs.*
4 du Gay et al., *Doing Cultural Studies.*
5 For an in depth analysis of live music see: Anderton and Pisfil, *Researching Live Music: Gigs, Tours, Concerts and Festivals.*

other workers, and themselves.[6] We don't see the people who make music before our eyes; they are hidden from view. Because of this alienation, people begin to believe any number of false ideas about people who make music. First, alienation leads to the belief that all signed artists are rich. The reality is most struggle to put food on the table.[7] Second, there is the myth that record contracts are a means to success.[8] Meanwhile, most musicians who sign a record contract, not only rarely make money, but they also often have their albums shelved—meaning the album is never brought to market. Finally, the myth of the autonomous artist obscures the reality of corporate control.[9] In this myth, artists need freedom from a boss to be able to write and perform music. Sara Bareilles shows the seductiveness of this myth in "Love Song," where she excoriates her record label for taking away artistic autonomy by demanding specific music (i.e., write a love song).[10] As part of a social process, we must always understand recorded music is the result of networks of people.[11] New technologies appear to do something to music, but music is performed, produced, and distributed by people, often under the logic of corporations.

There are competing interests within the recorded music ecosystem. First, record labels compete for music listeners' attention. Second, record labels compete with other aspects of the music industry from music publishers to live music venues. Finally, corporate interests compete with independent and/or non-commercial interests. In all three instances, competition is a result of capitalism as labels vie for profits. Music doesn't matter, money matters. While labels compete against each other, musicians compete with other musicians to show their quality as ingrained by a system of performance competition instilled through the logics of music training—i.e., chair tests, auditions, high school band competitions, battle of the bands.[12] As a system motivated by profit, major record labels view every change in society as an opportunity to drive more revenue and create surplus value.

Recorded music is a commodity produced by record labels to generate profit. Record labels create profit because they own the means of production and employ musicians to record music. The means of production are the

---

6 Marx, "Economic and Philosophic Manuscripts of 1844."
7 Arditi, "Musicians, Labor, and COVID19."; Slichter, *So You Wanna Be a Rock & Roll Star: How I Machine-Gunned a Roomful of Record Executives and Other True Tales from a Drummer's Life.*
8 Arditi, *Getting Signed.*
9 Marshall, *Bootlegging.*
10 Bareilles, *Love Song.*
11 Becker, *Art Worlds.*
12 Arditi, "On Competition in Music."

tools, money, and raw material it takes to produce things. Music is an odd commodity because the means of production costs very little to make music. To make music, musicians only need an instrument, but to make recorded music, they need studio equipment and other workers (engineers, producers, etc.). Recording technology created a system whereby capital could exploit labor by changing the musical commodity and industrializing the production of music.

From the perspective of record labels, every technological and cultural change in society presents a problem because music could become a non-commodified cultural good once again. This book is about the ways record labels use their power to ensure new social institutions and technologies do not threaten their existence. At each shift, record labels utilize corporate power to lobby legislators, fight in courts, and persuade the public that music's existence depends on people buying music from them.

In this book, I engage what I call the "piracy panic narrative," which is the story record labels tell us about scary music pirates: copying music is piracy, piracy is stealing, and stealing hurts the very artists who music fans love.[13] I developed the piracy panic narrative from the recording industry's reaction to file-sharing programs such as Napster and KaZaA, but here I look at the broader context of the piracy panic narrative from composers and publishers in the nineteenth century to social media and artificial intelligence (AI) today. The moral panics around music present a rich discourse to analyze the manifestations of power during unique moments of recording distribution. While the folk devil at each moment is ostensibly the people violating copyright and/or distribution norms, the real problem for major labels is the alternative music that arises alongside the conventional popular music commodity. New media forms of recording and distribution offer independent musicians the opportunity to release their music in ways unavailable before. It then becomes the mission of major record labels to eliminate avenues of distribution by their would-be competitors. They do so by attacking fans for their preferred forms of consumption and concealing their actual agenda from the public. If people are listening to indie music, they're not listening to major label music. It doesn't matter if the independent music is profitable or not because there is only so much listening time, and everyone is competing for that time. By listening to non-major label music, indie music listeners hurt the industry's bottom line. Therefore, these listeners

---

13 Arditi, *iTake-Over*; Arditi, "Downloading Is Killing Music"; Arditi, "Policing Piracy: The Piracy Panic Narrative from Napster to Spotify."

are a scourge that must be stopped, but they cannot eliminate this type of listening by being honest and competing for attention.

Panic Narratives

Fear drives policy.[14] If people are afraid of something, they look for someone or something to protect them.[15] As such, the powerful have incentive to construct moral panics to help create policy and social outcomes favorable to their interests. The vacuum left by fear can be filled with policies.

There is a long history of constructing social deviants and political opponents as folk devils in panic narratives dating back to the Salem witch trials in the United States. In *Folk Devils and Moral Panics*,[16] Stanley Cohen provides an account of the ways through which people who do not adhere to societal norms become demonized. While Cohen's work is on youth subcultures, his theories apply to a much broader range of deviants. Cohen illustrates this:

> A condition, episode, person or group of persons emerges to become defined as a threat to societal values and interests; its nature is presented in a stylized and stereotypical fashion by the mass media; the moral barricades are manned by editors, bishops, politicians and other right-thinking people; socially accredited experts pronounce their diagnoses and solutions; ways of coping are evolved or (more often) resorted to; the condition then disappears, submerges or deteriorates and becomes more visible.[17]

In a similar way, copyright pirates emerge as a threat to intellectual property ownership. News outlets stereotype copyright pirates as deviant for failing to follow the established norms to consume music through legitimated means. Politicians and the powerful[18] construct the moral parameters of piracy. Think tanks and trade associations act as experts on the issue. Meanwhile,

---

14 Parts of this section first appeared in Arditi, "Downloading Is Killing Music."
15 Horkheimer and Adorno, *Dialectic of Enlightenment*.
16 Cohen, *Folk Devils and Moral Panics: The Creation of the Mods and Rockers*.
17 Cohen, *Folk Devils and Moral Panics: The Creation of the Mods and Rockers*, 1.
18 Metallica's very public crusade against file-sharing is ironic because as Rob Drew explains, Metallica became popular as a result of the "heavy metal tape-trading network" (Drew, "New Technologies and the Business of Music: Lessons from the 1980s Home Taping Hearings," 9.). Drew contends that Metallica actively benefited from avoiding major labels and the copyright system in 1982 by trading their tapes.

the music industry provides a parallel non-deviant form of consumption (e.g., iTunes) for those who do not want to be perceived as deviant.

If the problem were limited to accusations of piracy, then the moral panic itself would receive little traction (i.e., who cares if people copy music?); however, the recording industry uses moral panics to legislate and litigate pirates. Erich Goode and Nachman Ben-Yehuda claim that moral panics are inherently political as different power holders attempt to negotiate the legal system by labeling particular behaviors as deviant.[19] "Designating certain acts as criminal serves at least three functions," Goode and Ben-Yehuda explain, "first, it *legitimates* a certain category's definition of right and wrong; second, it *symbolizes* the respectability of one category *vis-à-vis* another; and third, it *punishes* members of one category for engaging in behavior [...]"[20] A moral panic is needed to define music copiers in the first two functions, but before the state can punish people for a criminal offense, the activity must be crime. In turn, powerful interests use the moral panic to create the legal structure to punish pirates as stakeholders attempt "to crystallize [their] views into the legal structure – to pass laws compatible with, or prevent the passage of laws incompatible with, its own ideological, moral, and political-economic system."[21] The piracy panic narrative is used to change music listening habits and modify the laws that govern those habits.

Beyond constructing a panic about a particular activity, panic narratives stem from a moral position. Not only are pirates out there lurking on computers in dark rooms with Cheetos crumbs on their keyboards, but an article in *Rolling Stone* magazine says they could be your churchgoing (i.e., morally upstanding) neighbor.[22] Julian Dibbell presents the recording industry's digital pirate as:

> the music lover who simply sees no point in paying for recorded music. Until now this person was typically found on college campuses, where massive bandwidth and wide-open networks have long encouraged undergraduates to seek their music not in megastores but on their peers' hard drives. But as DSL and cable modems bring high-speed Web access to the masses and as programs like Napster simplify the online file-sharing process, the non-CD-buying music fan is increasingly popping up in other demographics.[23]

---

19 Goode and Ben-Yehuda, *Moral Panics*.
20 Goode and Ben-Yehuda, *Moral Panics*, 119.
21 Goode and Ben-Yehuda, *Moral Panics*, 120.
22 Dibbell, "The New Face of Music Piracy."
23 Dibbell, "The New Face of Music Piracy."

The protagonist of Dibbell's story is Mary Long, a woman who Dibbell describes as a "churchgoing" woman who teaches preschool at her church. Long is quoted in the article after being asked if she worries about the ethics of downloading music "Oh, sometimes – but I get over it."[24] By pointing to a woman who teaches preschool at a church, *Rolling Stone* asserts Long is a highly moral person[25]; this is an appeal to morality that is the archetype of a moral panic since morality is "a view of right and wrong."[26] Therefore, what Dibbell implies is that there is a well-founded ethical position behind being against file-sharing. However, not only does piracy lack a clear-cut ethical position, but the term itself is a dubious substitute for an actual legal category (copyright infringement) that may not even be relevant to Long's downloading practices.

Yet the piracy panic narrative is never specific about what constitutes piracy. What is piracy? The next section will provide a brief overview of piracy or rather what is claimed to be piracy.

Piracy

Pirates are bad people. Stories of Blackbeard cruising the Atlantic, lighting fuses in his beard, and robbing ships stoke the fear of pirates. In popular culture, pirates represent universally bad people who attempt to steal ships from *Star Wars* to *Guardians of the Galaxy*. In the contemporary Indian Ocean, Somali pirates board ships to hold the ships and their crew for ransom.[27] The symbol of pirates is the Jolly Roger: a black flag with a skull and crossbones. Pirates have no respect for humanity and cause big problems with international law and order. As such anything labeled as "piracy," represents an abhorrent activity.[28]

Yet piracy has a very limited legal definition. In the United States of America, piracy is defined in Title 18, Chapter 81 of the United States Code and only applies to robbery, murder, and other crimes that happen in the "high seas." But in the popular imaginary, piracy also deals with violation of copyright laws.

This can be seen before the recording era as publishers and composers criticized the illegal copying of sheet music. John Philip Sousa wrote a letter to the editor of the *Daily Mail* in 1905 criticizing the perceived negligence

---

24 Dibbell, "The New Face of Music Piracy."
25 Miller, "Diminished Citizenship."
26 Goode and Ben-Yehuda, *Moral Panics*, 110.
27 Ahmed, "Somali Piracy 2.0 – the Angry Fishermen on the High Seas."
28 Sinnreich, *The Piracy Crusade*; Burkart, *Pirate Politics*.

of laws in the United Kingdom. He states, "Because of the laxity of your laws, and because of the perseverance of your music pirates, my royalties have gone a-glimmering."[29] The irony is that the United States did not become party to international copyright until 1891.[30] Before 1891, US publishers would print British books without paying for copyright permissions, which flooded the US market with cheap books.[31] To compete with cheap British books, American authors had to devise a uniquely American style of writing to attract audiences, like Mark Twain.[32] But as soon as the US government began enforcing international copyright, American authors shifted to the generic conventions of British authors. However, a mere 14 years later, Sousa is incredulous that publishers would print copyrighted music without permission. Sousa's language in his letter to the editor emphasizes that these printers act like Robin Hood, taking from the rich and giving to the poor, but he says their acts hurt the very artists who write the music. Here is the trope I analyze throughout this book: by pirating music, people hurt the very musicians they love.

When we discuss "piracy," most people think of illegally downloading movies or music, making photocopies of a book, or recording a movie with a camcorder. But legally speaking, piracy doesn't mean breaking copyright law. As mentioned above, US law only recognizes piracy in the traditional sense—attacking ships at sea (18 USC, Chapter 81). Yet, the term "piracy" is widely used by politicians, industry representatives, academics,[33] and even the FBI to describe copyright infringement. The FBI has an "Anti-Piracy Warning" seal that states: "The unauthorized reproduction or distribution of a copyrighted work is illegal. Criminal copyright infringement, including infringement without monetary gain, is investigated by the FBI and is punishable by fines and federal imprisonment."[34] However, the label "Anti-Piracy" is misleading. The warning describes copyright infringement, but the warning doesn't mention piracy. It also implies infringement can happen "without monetary gain." US copyright law, specifically Title 17 USC §1008, makes it clear that copyright infringement is tied to commerce. In other words, noncommercial copying by consumers—like making a personal copy of a song—doesn't count as infringement under the law.

---

29 Sousa, "Letter to the Editor of the 'Daily Mail.'"
30 Association of Research Libraries, "Copyright Timeline."
31 Grazian, *Mix It Up*.
32 Vaidhyanathan, *Copyrights and Copywrongs*.
33 Al-Rafee and Cronan, "Digital Piracy."
34 FBI, "Download the FBI's Anti-Piracy Warning Seal."

This isn't just an issue in the United States. International law also sticks to the traditional meaning of piracy—attacks on ships, not photocopying a book. As Suzannah Mirghani points out, "The absence of the words 'piracy' and 'pirate' from these texts of international copyright law [...] can only mean that the semantic association of the word 'piracy' with 'copyright infringement' is a discourse formation that has occurred largely outside of official copyright law."[35] In other words, the way we link piracy to copyright infringement is a cultural position, not a legal reality.

So why is "piracy" used so often in this context? It's part of a moral panic fueled by the copyright industry. Since noncommercial copying isn't technically infringement, they frame unauthorized copying as theft, arguing that every copied song or movie represents lost revenue. But this argument relies on a major misconception: copyright isn't a property right. As William Patry expounds, copyright has always been a regulatory privilege, not ownership of an object or idea.[36] The industry, however, uses strong language—like calling file-sharers "pirates"—to paint them as villains in a black-and-white moral battle.[37]

The truth is, when someone copies a song, they don't "steal" anything. The only way to truly steal copyrighted material is to take the physical copy, which falls under property law—not copyright law. So, the widespread use of "piracy" in discussions about copyright isn't based on law, but on a constructed narrative designed to reinforce industry interests.

Music Panic Narratives

Music panic narratives are as old as the phonograph. Different people and institutions have used panic narratives to attempt to change the hearts and minds of the public and politicians. By creating folk devils, interests within the music industry can shape policy and law.

At the turn of the twentieth century, John Philip Sousa was livid about the phonograph replacing home musical instruments. "The cheaper of these instruments of the home are no longer being purchased as formerly, and all because the automatic music devices are usurping their places."[38] In the nineteenth century, people needed to learn to play an instrument to have music in the home. They needed to learn to sing and play piano or guitar. Sousa worried that people would stop learning to play instruments

---

35 Mirghani, "The War on Piracy," 117.
36 Patry, *Moral Panics and the Copyright Wars*, 110.
37 Patry, *Moral Panics and the Copyright Wars*, 91.
38 Sousa, "The Menace of Mechanical Music."

because they owned a cheap phonograph. As people stopped learning to play instruments, Sousa claimed the effects would be felt throughout society, especially by musician workers because musicians would no longer be needed to teach music lessons or perform at restaurants.

The issues around labor are real, but the hysteria about the future of music making shared by Sousa, and others, was overblown because people keep making music despite the changes. The same narrative has been repeated over the years. From DJs to Digital Audio Workstations (DAWs), people claimed the addition of a new technology would not only change music, but also threaten music's very existence. Recorded music did presage significant changes. For instance, the addition of recorded music to movies created an upheaval for musician labor across the United States as labor became alienated through film music production in Los Angeles; this led to widespread lay-offs for musicians at theaters.[39] Restaurants and bars introduced jukeboxes and DJs for the performance of music, thereby reducing the number of gigs available for musicians, not to mention the impact on party bands at weddings and bar/bat mitzvahs.

A similar phenomenon to Sousa's fear about the declining number of employed musicians occurred in the 2010s. People wrote about the end of the guitar[40] alongside the overall decline of rock music. While there may have been some decline in the United States, the guitar did not die.[41] When COVID hit, people were stuck at home, and there was a surge in guitar sales as people decided to spend their spare time at home learning guitar.[42] The demand for guitar lessons in a socially distanced world led to the rise of Zoom guitar lessons and online tutorials.[43] It turns out that there is something deeply cultural about learning music that no matter the changes wrought by technology, people continue to play music.

At other times, genres of music induced panic. Rock & Roll emerged at a time of social transformation in the United States. Following World War II, a new emphasis grew on "youth culture."[44] Rock & Roll emphasized everything in American society that scared conservative power: rebellion,

---

39 Kelley, "Without a Song: New York Musicians Strike Out against Technology"; Kraft, "Musicians in Hollywood: Work and Technological Change in Entertainment Industries, 1926–1940."
40 McCarthy, "End of the Guitar?"
41 Wang, "Guitars Aren't Dying. They're as Popular as Ever."
42 Hissong, "Did Everyone Buy a Guitar in Quarantine or What?"
43 Cording, "Study Shows 16 Million People Learned to Play Guitar during the First Two Years of the Pandemic."
44 Hall and Jefferson, *Resistance Through Rituals: Youth Subcultures in Post-War Britain.*

race, and sexuality. As young people embraced the music, parents decried it as the "devil's music." The fear of Rock & Roll perpetuated the idea that it ran counter to Christian teachings. This happened again with hip-hop. At first, there were attacks from people saying rap wasn't music because of the use of DJs and rapping instead of singing. As hip-hop music became more popular, a shift occurred from questions about the musicality to issues of violence and sexuality. Bill Clinton infamously confronted Sister Souljah for remarks she made about violence following the LA riots.[45] There were widespread legal attacks on 2 Live Crew because some people thought their lyrics were obscene.[46] The rise of gangsta rap, which was primarily produced to market to white suburban boys,[47] led to many attacks on hip-hop music. And hip-hop was continually attacked for the use of sampling copyrighted material.[48]

There are numerous other moments when powerful interests constructed specific acts of musical performance as morally repugnant. This included the explicit use of "pirate" in pirate radio.

Book Outline

While music panic narratives go back to at least the nineteenth century, this book begins with the tape cassette because of its importance, both symbolic and political, to the recording industry. From the outset, tape cassettes threatened the business model in the recording industry. Chapter 2 explores the ways the recording industry addressed the adaptation of tape cassettes by music fans. Tapes provided an easy portable mechanism to store, copy, and distribute music. On the one hand, this created a new moment for the album-replacement cycle where fans who already owned music on vinyl repurchased the same music to listen on tape cassettes. On the other hand, the technology permitted fans to make copies of their vinyl records without re-purchasing the music. Record labels and their trade organizations fought the technology most famously with the British Phonographic Industry's "Home taping is killing music" campaign and lawsuits such as *Sony Corp. of America v. Universal City Studios, Inc* (aka., the Betamax case). This chapter follows these issues through the 1990s to issues with CD-RWs.

---

45 Broder and Edsall, "Clinton Finds Biracial Support for Criticism of Rap Singer."
46 Harrell, "2 Live Crew Fought the Law with Its Album, 'As Nasty As They Wanna Be.'"
47 Watkins, *Hip Hop Matters: Politics, Pop Culture, and the Struggle for the Soul of a Movement*.
48 McLeod, "Intellectual Property Law, Freedom of Expression, and the Web."

Following the release of Napster in 1999, the piracy panic narrative hit its apex. In Chapter 3, I provide the reader with context on the way major labels and their trade organizations fought to stop file-sharing. The strategy was to portray musicians as victims of theft at the hands of their own fans. The chapter begins by describing Napster and the legal quagmire that followed led by Metallica and the RIAA. After Napster's demise, a number of file-sharing services developed, followed by bit-torrents. Finally, I show the RIAA began suing file-sharers at the same time it began pushing iTunes and the download era.

Chapter 4 analyzes the piracy panic narrative beyond piracy. While bit-torrents were still popular tools in the 2010s, streaming services unseated the prominence of piracy. Streaming music provided a new folk devil for the recording industry, but it was one with nuance. Instead of claiming music fans were killing music through piracy, record labels and music trade organizations shifted to a position that encouraged subscriptions through their preferred platforms. I describe the "value gap" as the panic narrative of the era where the RIAA and the IFPI contended that specific forms of ad-supported streaming devalued renumeration to artists. Interestingly, record labels are unconcerned about the failed renumeration of songwriters on streaming platforms.

In the conclusion, I provide the context of the overall piracy panic narrative to show that at each moment of potential change and disruption, the recording industry has publicly decried the threat of new technologies while working in the background to benefit from them. First, I address the ways major record labels killed music from the sound of music to valuing appearance over the sound of music. Next, I explore the way the recording industry has deployed the piracy panic narrative to attack AI. Labels and trade organizations warn of the unauthorized use of copyrighted material to train AI software. However, in the background, they are developing their own AI services to undercut musicians in the production process.

Music panic narratives are rhetorical constructions used to advance the interests of the major record labels. They aim to make music listeners question their actions and support the recording industry's profit models in the name of the artists they love. This book aims to push back against these narratives to help give music listeners the power to resist this system.

Chapter 2

TAPE CASSETTES AND BLANK CDS: HOME TAPING IS KILLING MUSIC

In 1981, with five words by the British Phonographic Industry (BPI), the recording industry launched the piracy panic narrative: "Home taping is killing music." To drive the point home, the slogan appeared above a Jolly Roger where a tape cassette replaced the skull above the crossbones, and they added "and it's illegal" below for good measure. By inculcating a sense of immorality, crime, and violence alongside the death of music, BPI hoped to implicate music fans as hurting the musicians they loved.

Whereas vinyl records (and cylinders before them) could not be reproduced at home, tape cassettes provided easily writable and rewritable media to consumers. This was enabled not only by the cassettes, but also the players. Tape decks and boomboxes came with a "record" button enabling owners to turn into reproducers. Music fans taped the radio. They taped records. They taped other tapes. This led to the practice of "re-recording"—what David Morton used to refer to the duplication of commercial music.[1] Tape cassettes enabled cultural practices hitherto unavailable to music fans.

Blank media was an easy folk devil. In previous mediations, the costly equipment necessary to print copies made it cost prohibitive to copy and sell (i.e., pirate) music except for the largest commercial operations. Before the recording era, the means of production for music constituted primarily of the musical instruments used to perform music. Following the introduction of recording technology, the nascent record labels used copyrights to separate musicians from their means of production.[2] Copyrights had value deployed by labels to ensure money could be made from music. Musicians were willing to sell their copyrights in exchange for an advance to record their music.[3] This process divorced musicians from their copyrights and

---

1 Morton, *Off the Record*, 36.
2 Arditi, "Digital Downsizing."
3 Arditi, *Getting Signed*.

amplified the importance of recordings for musicians to earn a living. With the entrenchment of copyrights, the cost of the means of production also inhibited independent artists from entering the market without the same capital investments as majors or commercial pirates. Tape cassettes changed the way music is produced, distributed, and consumed by lowering the cost of the means of production for recorded music, but major record labels wanted to maintain their business model despite the changes.

Record labels fought this battle on two fronts. First, they tried to shape the discourse by labeling home tapers "pirates" (discussed above). Second, they took a legal approach. This was adjudicated in the courts in the 1984 Betamax Case (*Sony Corp. of America v. Universal City Studios, Inc., 464 U.S. 417*). Hollywood fought Sony's Betamax video tapes for perceived piracy of live broadcasts. However, the US Supreme Court sided with Sony and established that "time shifting" was an acceptable practice covered by the fair use doctrine. Time shifting is the practice of recording something live, over the air, to watch at a more convenient time. This applied to both television and radio. The legal approach concluded when the recording industry enshrined in law a royalty on the sale of blank digital media through the Audio Home Recording Act of 1992. While the recording industry failed to stop rerecording, they did ensure a royalty would be paid to record labels for digital blank media.

However, the recording industry's contention that tape cassettes—and later blank compact discs (CDs)—were killing music stands in stark contrast to the types of cultural creation the format enabled from mixtapes to tape trading.[4] Technology provides affordances, which means people create technologies for specific reasons. Those affordances enable or disable cultural practices. In the case of tape cassettes and other blank media, the result was allowing people to mix and remix the music they enjoyed sharing with friends, family, and significant others. By ascribing criminality to the use of tape cassettes for rerecording, the major record labels and their trade group partners aimed to limit cultural practices. Viewed from the perspective of music fans: home taping didn't kill music, but rather encouraged the mixing, remixing, and cultural diffusion of music.

---

4 Harrison, *Hip Hop Underground: The Integrity and Ethics of Racial Identification*; Harrison, "'Cheaper than a CD, plus We Really Mean It': Bay Area Underground Hip Hop Tapes as Subcultural Artifacts"; Burns, *Mixtape Nostalgia*; Drew, "New Technologies and the Business of Music: Lessons from the 1980s Home Taping Hearings"; Drew, *Unspooled*.

The piracy panic narrative facilitated major record labels to establish the rhetorical position of tape cassettes and rerecording in the popular imaginary. In the rhetoric about piracy, the major record labels concealed their concerns about two threats to their profits. First, tape cassettes interfered with the album-replacement cycle. The next section addresses the way labels relied on the periodic repurchasing of new music, so fans could hear their favorite music on new media. Tape cassettes represented the first threat to the album-replacement cycle. Second, tape cassettes provided an opportunity for independent artists to distribute music cheaply and compete with major labels over listener's attention. Here, I explore the rise of independent music as a threat to major label continued dominance.

End of the Album-Replacement Cycle

From the inception of recorded music, record labels have benefited from planned obsolescence—a business model where new products are developed to become obsolete on a short timeline. Thomas Edison's original phonograph used cylinders etched with grooves to make sound, while Emile Berliner's gramophone used a disc plate with grooves to produce sound. The Edison Phonograph Company quickly changed the phonograph to mimic Berliner's design, which meant that cylinder records couldn't be played on the new machines. Phonograph and Gramophone companies then began to develop better sounding machines that only played newer formats. As people began collecting music, they would want to hear their music on their new machines, meaning they would have to repurchase the music they owned already.

This was true beginning with the original 78-rounds per minute (rpm) records that dominated from roughly 1898 to the 1950s. The original gramophone spun at 78rpm and played a 10–12-inch disc. While there were incremental improvements to fidelity throughout the period, there weren't large-scale changes to the format that meant needing to replace one's music. One major change followed the establishment of the Recording Industry Association of America (RIAA), which was founded to standardize record players, so all records could be played on all record players. In the late 1940s, two formats were introduced to better utilize the improved recording techniques: the 33 1/3-rpm record in 1948 and the 45-rpm record in 1949. Both formats created better sound quality and offered greater storage capacity. Instead of the approximately 3 minutes of music per side permitted by the 78-rpm record, 45s and 33 1/3s allowed 15 and 22 minutes per side, respectively. Ultimately a settlement was arrived at where the 33 1/3 became the format of choice for long-play records and the 45 was the format for singles until labels stopped producing 45s in 1990.

As consumers purchased record players that played 45s and 33 1/3 records, they had to replace their catalog of 78s with the new formats. This led to the increase in catalog record sales. Catalog sales are those "sales of records that have been in the marketplace for over 18 months."[5] At the time consumers purchased music in both new formats, but far fewer 45s were sold until they ultimately stopped being produced in 1990. Then in 1957, stereophonic records became popular. At this junction, people may have already owned their music in the 33 1/3 (Long Play—i.e., LP) format, but the recording industry began the process of "remastering" records in stereo format. To remaster is to remix the sounds on the master recording, then print the new editions. For audiophiles, this was an excellent opportunity to repurchase their older record collection with new high-fidelity sound.

With every new sound recording playback device, the recording industry sees a bump in their catalog sales. David Park calls this process the "CD replacement cycle" in which the CD "was premised on the assumption that baby boomers would be likely to replace their vinyl collection with CDs."[6] Park emphasizes the position of CDs in the process. Aram Sinnreich calls it the format placement cycle, which helps to reframe the process as something older that arises from changes in format. I call this the "album-replacement cycle" to emphasize the content over the format. In other words, when people replace their collections, they aren't doing it to replace a specific format (e.g., vinyl), but to be able to listen to their favorite music in the newest format. When the recording industry adopts new recorded media formats, labels increase profits because consumers desire to hear the music they already own on their new music players.[7] With each new media, record labels expect to see an increase in revenues driven by music consumers repurchasing albums they already own in their collection because they boost catalog sales.

Every time a new recording format arrives, there is a lag before the technology becomes ubiquitous, but the early growth of a format by audiophiles amplifies the overall market for recorded music. Figure 2.1 shows global record shipments as reported by the International Federation of the Phonographic Industry (IFPI)—note, this is self-reported data that often overestimates total record sales.[8] Notice here the overall expansion

---

5 Hull, Hutchison, and Strasser, *The Music Business and Recording Industry: Delivering Music in the 21st Century*, 248.
6 Park, *Conglomerate Rock: The Music Industry's Quest to Divide Music and Conquer Wallets*, 72.
7 Sinnreich, *The Piracy Crusade*.
8 Arditi, *The Recording Industry in Numbers: A Record Label Centered View of Recorded Music*.

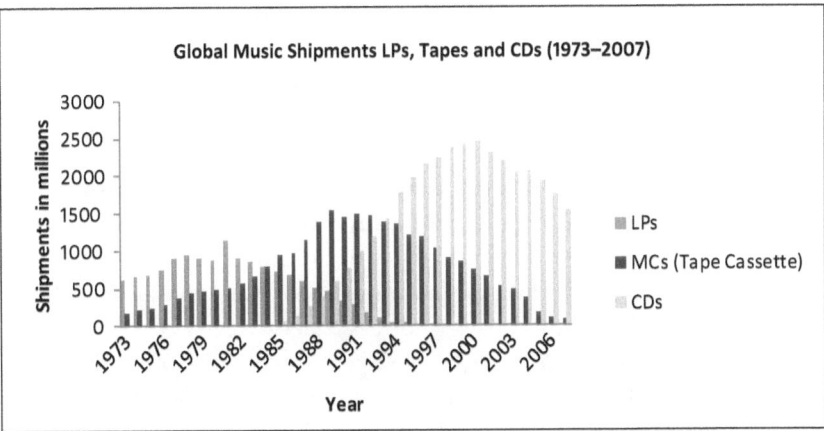

Figure 2.1 Global Record Shipments for LPs, Tapes, and CDs.

of the global recording industry with sales consistently increasing over time. With each new media format, the market expands. This is a strategy record labels use not only to sell new music, but also to make catalog sales.

At work is a process known as the expansion of the means of consumption, which developed as part of twentieth-century capitalism. Capitalism has periodic downturns where supply of commodities outpaces demand. Because there aren't consumers to buy a good, commodities sit in warehouses and capitalists layoff their workers. This causes an economic downturn. At the same time, affluent consumers have extra money they are willing to spend, but there aren't commodities for them to buy. The expansion of the means of consumption is a theory described by the regulation school, led by Michel Aglietta, that explains the way capitalism dealt with chronic oversupply of commodities.[9] This largely depended on the production and sale of leisure or luxury goods in the culture industry.[10]

The expansion of the means of consumption has a long history in the recording industry. After gramophone companies realized people liked to buy musical recordings to play on their gramophones, they began producing more musical recordings. Then the gramophone companies realized there is more revenue to be made from selling recordings instead of players. Gramophone

---

9 Aglietta, *A Theory of Capitalist Regulation*.
10 Horkheimer and Adorno, "The Culture Industry: Enlightenment as Mass Deception."

companies could only sell a limited number of gramophones because after a household owned one gramophone, they didn't see a reason to own more. However, if gramophone companies could continue to sell records to play on the machines, their sales could be virtually limitless. Eventually, gramophone companies became more identifiable by the labels they stuck to their records because these companies started focusing more on the content than the players; this led to them being known as record labels. The importance of music players to the recording industry is demonstrated by the IFPI, which continued to monitor the level of penetration and saturation for new media players well into the 2000s.[11]

The album-replacement cycle is an effective expansion of the means of consumption as it assures a steady inflow of cash to major record labels and publishers for every new media player. There is a degree of planned obsolescence here. Planned obsolescence is the intentional design of one item to force consumers to replace it with a newer product. The recording industry already benefited from people purchasing newly released music, but labels ensured further growth with each new format as music fans replaced their old collection in the new format.

This came crashing down, at least in theory, when consumer electronics companies began selling tape cassette players with a record function. Suddenly, music fans could rerecord the music they owned on vinyl to tape cassette. The advantage of tape cassettes emerged from their portability, not their sound quality. Whereas previous iterations of the album-replacement cycle increased sound fidelity, the tape cassette provided a lower-quality product than vinyl records. However, tape cassettes were a fraction of the size and cost of vinyl. Furthermore, cassettes could be played in cars and on the move without skipping. With the invention of the Sony Walkman in 1979, cassettes allowed people to listen to music anywhere.[12] Yet, record labels worried they would no longer be able to count on people repurchasing music they owned if they could rerecord their music by connecting their record players to their tape decks using an RCA cable.

---

11 IFPI, "Recording Industry in Numbers," 2003; IFPI, "Recording Industry in Numbers," 2004; IFPI, "Recording Industry in Numbers," 2005; Arditi, *The Recording Industry in Numbers: A Record Label Centered View of Recorded Music*; Arditi, "The Global Music Report: Selling a Narrative of Decline."

12 du Gay et al., *Doing Cultural Studies*.

While the IFPI did not report catalog sales during the rise of tape cassettes, the growth of cassette consumption was slower than other formats.[13] From 1973 to 1983, cassettes grew from 185 million units to 660 million units in sales.[14] Cassette sales equaled vinyl for the first time in 1984 at 800 million units and surpassed records for the first time in 1985 (see Figure 2.1).[15] Vinyl sales peaked at 1.14 billion units in 1981,[16] which means people preferred vinyl well into the 1980s. Nonetheless, tapes presented an existential threat to the album-replacement cycle through the 1980s until compact discs (CDs) took hold of the market in the early 1990s because people could so easily rerecord their music collections.

CDs provided a brief respite to the album-replacement cycle. While cassettes suffered from poor sound quality and physical fragility,[17] CDs offered the highest fidelity commercially available and a much smaller size than vinyl. Classical music aficionados were especially enamored with the fidelity of CDs. Consumers were slow to adopt CDs in the early years, but they provided a boon for record label catalogs. If people wanted to hear their music on CD, they had to purchase it in the format. Whereas tape cassettes could be used for rerecording, there were not commercially available compact disc-recordable (CD-R) machines until the 1990s. In fact, the commercial availability of CD-Rs was not widespread until the compact disc-rewritable (CD-RW) became available on CD-ROMs in 1999. Until the boom of CD-RW drives on computers, consumers had to purchase a separate CD-R machine to record their collections.

Digital technology permitted the home reproduction of music without any loss of fidelity from copying. If anyone can reproduce music from one format to another format, they could rerecord their entire record collection from one format to another with relatively cheap and readily available technology. Since digital files can be reproduced easily at home, record labels lost their ability to control the adoption of music into new formats. This tension first appeared following the creation of the Digital Audio Tape (DAT) recorder. DAT recorders gave users the ability to make copies of copies without any fidelity loss. The recording industry feared widespread commercial availability of these devices would lead to extensive "piracy."

---

13 IFPI, "Recording Industry in Numbers," 2000; IFPI, "Recording Industry in Numbers," 2010.
14 IFPI, "Recording Industry in Numbers," 2000.
15 Ibid.
16 Ibid.
17 Drew, "New Technologies and the Business of Music: Lessons from the 1980s Home Taping Hearings."

Congress passed the Audio Home Recording Rights Act (AHRA) of 1992 to deal with this digital reproduction. The AHRA mandated the inclusion of Digital Rights Management (DRM) that created loss of sound fidelity for copies of copies, and it required consumer electronics manufacturers to pay royalties to the RIAA for digital recording media designed for recording music.

Since digital players were equipped with a record button, the recording industry wanted to make DAT players illegal, so they threatened not to issue licenses to the copyrights they controlled for DAT music. Record labels and publishers agreed to make digital players legal in exchange for royalties "on every digital recording device player and digital tape sold."[18] The AHRA requires DAT machines to be made to recognize computer code that would downgrade the quality of each respective copy to make DATs more similar to tape cassettes. When the code on the digital recording identifies a recording as a copy of a copy, it records the music at a progressively lower fidelity for each consecutive recording.[19] This marks the first time record collectors lost the ability to do what they wanted with their record collections. If labels were concerned about commercial reproduction (i.e., piracy), then they would have developed a larger royalty on commercial sized digital copying machines. By insisting on royalties on blank media, the recording industry demonstrated their desire to reclaim revenue lost from the album-replacement cycle rather than commercial reproduction.

Even though the AHRA only pertains to DAT and DAT recorders, the Fairness in Music Licensing Act of 1998 updated the law to apply to CDs. Under the updated provisions, blank CDs labeled for music and stand-alone CD burners had royalties levied on their sale, regardless of whether they were used to record copyrighted material.

Independent Record Production

Major record labels depend on consumers purchasing music they want to hear for a market price usually set by the industry. Whether the industry sells tapes, 78s, LPs (33 1/3 records), or CDs most albums for sale in a record store are the same price—new releases may be $14.99, while catalog albums may be $9.99. In other words, price wasn't set by demand. The same remains true with digital downloads and streaming subscriptions. Since major labels have large marketing budgets and control the distribution channels,[20] they have

---

18 Litman, *Digital Copyright*, 61.
19 Lessig, *Code*.
20 Krasilovsky et al., *This Business of Music*; Frith, "The Industrialization of Popular Music."

the power to influence consumer demand and get their music into stores (or now on playlists). This means that (a) consumers with expendable money to buy records drive demand; and (b) only musicians supported by the industry (for whatever reason) make it to fans. Tapes intervened by allowing music consumers to circulate music cheaply and giving musicians a cheap medium to distribute/circulate their music. As a result, tape cassettes enabled cultural practices that threatened the major labels' business model.

People have always made music as part of their culture—this is why the idea of "killing music" is complete hyperbole. But culture is neither some singular thing we put in museums nor general characteristics ascribed to a group of people. Culture is the process through which people make symbolic meaning out of everyday things. Music is used by people to organize noise[21] into symbolically important sounds. Rather than killing music, tape cassettes enabled new cultural practices with symbolic significance far beyond the profits of major record labels.

Tape cassettes enabled people (especially youths) to share the music they were passionate about with their friends, family, and acquaintances. They could tape music from the radio. They could tape music from their vinyl collection. They could tape themselves playing music. They could compile different recordings on a mixtape.[22] Taping music became its own cultural phenomenon, but one that threatened the bottom line of record labels.

Buried in the fear of easily copied music was the unique usage where independent artists could easily distribute music to fans. If musicians wanted to tape music at home and distribute it to their fans, they could do so without large budgets for studio time and marketing. However, outlawing home taping would force consumer electronics to change the technology. In which case, the unique usage for independent music production—a practice that is entirely legal—would have become more difficult because musicians would have to purchase expensive reproduction technologies. This would have made it difficult for musicians to get their music to listeners, again limiting who can make music and once again enabling profits for major record labels.

Tape cassettes gave power to working-class and marginalized groups to produce and circulate counterhegemonic music because it interrupted previous costly means of production. Hegemony is the dominant power in society that exercises power and control for the dominant class in society—it

---

21 Attali, *Noise: The Political Economy of Music*.
22 Harrison, "'Cheaper than a CD, plus We Really Mean It': Bay Area Underground Hip Hop Tapes as Subcultural Artifacts"; Burns, *Mixtape Nostalgia*; Drew, *Unspooled*.

usually operates through culture. Most music produced by the major record labels produces and reinforces hegemonic power. Major labels use their capital and the means of production to advance both their position in the wider music landscape and the interests of capitalism more generally.[23] Counterhegemony is an articulation of ideology outside of the dominant class; it opposes power at its core.[24] Counterhegemonic music may provide discourse outside of the dominant political ideology, but more importantly, it gives those disaffected by the system a place to create and share meanings (i.e. culture). These messages may not be popular with the major record labels, but that is not the reason why the labels don't produce them. First, they need a wealthy consumer base with the income to buy the music they produce. If the music isn't palatable to a wide swath of the population, labels will not be able to sell much music. Second, they can only release so much music to make a profit. Every recording produced and distributed by major labels takes a large investment. Labels want to make sure they recoup their investment. At the same time, listeners only have so much time to listen to music. If a person listens to an independent artist on an independently released tape cassette, they aren't listening to a major label release. As a result, independent music directly threatens the labels' revenues and profits.

After computers began coming with CD-RW drives standard around 2000, the practice of self-recorded music distribution increased even further. However, even these CDs generated revenue for record labels because of the AHRA and the Fairness in Music Licensing Act. These laws assume record labels have a right to revenue generated from the sales of blank music CDs even if those CDs burned music of their competitors. Record labels used the piracy panic narrative in the tape era to deter use of tape cassettes by independent artists.

Conclusion

Who is killing music? Major record labels tried to kill music. The chapter started with BPI's claim that *you're* killing music. With the attacks on blank media (cassettes and CDs), the only people "killing music" in 1980s and 1990s were major labels and their trade organizations.

They tried to kill music on two fronts. First, they wanted to stop rerecording at home. While tapes, and later CDs, made it easy for record collectors to

---

23 Gramsci, "Hegemony, Relations of Force, Historical Bloc."
24 Laclau and Mouffe, *Hegemony and Socialist Strategy: Towards a Radical Democratic Politics.*

transition from LPs to the more portable cassettes, major record labels feared the loss of the album-replacement cycle. Even if record collectors wanted to re-purchase their music in a new format, music would not be universally available on cassettes. Record labels had to print and distribute catalog music to record stores. If an album wasn't available through this process, the music would disappear on new media. Since culture is a process, younger musicians would be unable to hear older music to help them create new music.

Second, by attempting to stop taping practices, major record labels tried to kill independent music—i.e., their competitors. Taping provided a cheap and accessible way for independent musicians to distribute their music to their fans. This was music produced by musicians who retained their copyrights—it wasn't piracy at all. Yet the harm for major labels was still financial. If fans listened to independent music instead of major label music, the major labels lost revenue. By insisting tape cassettes were a reprehensible technology, major labels associated the practice of independent musicians to distribute their own music as entirely illegal.

Chapter 3

NAPSTER: FILE-SHARING IS KILLING MUSIC

> Once in awhile, maybe you will feel the urge
> To break international copyright law
> By downloading MP3s from file-sharing sites
> Like Morpheus, or Grokster, or LimeWire, or Kazaa
> But deep in your heart, you know the guilt would drive you mad
> And the shame would leave a permanent scar
> 'Cause you start out stealing songs, then you're robbing liquor stores
> And selling crack and running over school kids with your car
>
> —"Don't Download this Song" by Weird Al Yankovic[1]

When Napster launched in 1999, it began the biggest music distribution panic narrative. In Weird Al Yankovic's framing, downloading music is a gateway crime that leads to much more heinous crimes. While Yankovic's satirical view of file-sharing emphasizes the immorality of such hardened criminals, the panic narrative spawned by the Recording Industry Association of America (RIAA), the International Federation of the Phonographic Industry (IFPI), major record labels, and celebrity musicians created a hysteria about the Internet that in some ways overshadowed the Dot.Com Bubble of the turn of the century. There was money to be made on the Internet, but not from music.

While a piracy panic narrative existed around tape cassettes, the industry rhetoric about file-sharing music made the threat of downloading music feel more existential. Tapes had some redeemable characteristics (i.e., portability and the album-replacement cycle) according to labels, but the RIAA insisted file-sharing only existed as a crime. According to the recording industry, there were no legitimate uses for file-sharing or downloading music (at least until

---

1 Yankovic, *Don't Download This Song*.

the iTunes Store launched). The piracy panic narrative holds that file-sharing is piracy, piracy is stealing music, and stealing music hurts recording artists. Their logic claimed downloading music was no different from walking out of a record store with a CD without paying for it. The "category of 'piracy' is used to associate file-sharing with organized crime and with illegal immigration."[2] Record labels felt like they had to frame file-sharing in such dire circumstances because downloading music was so easy.

The point they left out was that (1) non-commercial file-sharing isn't against the law, and (2) this was yet again a way to kill independent music. But in a way those issues are beside the point because the RIAA treated file-sharing as if it was the bubonic plague. First, the RIAA sued the file-sharing services, as with the landmark case *A&M Records, Inc. v. Napster, Inc.*[3] Then with the advent of iTunes, they began to sue users with the explicit goal of converting file-sharers to digital song buyers.[4] As Weird Al sang, "Oh, you don't want to mess with the R-I-double-A/They'll sue you if you burn that CD-R/It doesn't matter if you're a grandma or a seven-year-old girl/They'll treat you like the evil, hard bitten, criminal scum you are."[5] In truth, they sued several grandmothers, including an 83-year old who had passed away,[6] and a 12-year-old girl for $150 million.[7] The outlandish lawsuits claimed that each download (actually upload) had a value of $150,000 for damages.

In this chapter, first, I provide a description of the menace that Napster wrought on music. Then I turn to the position of musicians in the piracy panic narrative. While the RIAA claims music piracy is not a victimless crime and stated musicians were the victims, the RIAA deemphasized their real concern was the recording industry's dominant business model. Finally, I discuss the very real panic about decreasing CD sales. The RIAA and record labels claimed file-sharing was killing music, but the decrease in CD sales can be linked to the loss of the album-replacement cycle and changes in distribution. By labeling file-sharers as deviant criminals, the RIAA, IFPI, and major record labels protected their industry from change, competition, and criticism.

---

2 David, *Peer to Peer and the Music Industry*, 97.
3 Patel, A&M Records, Inc. v. Napster, Inc.
4 Arditi, *iTake-Over*.
5 Yankovic, *Don't Download This Song*.
6 Bangeman, "'I Sue Dead People [...].'"
7 Pham, "N.Y. Girl Settles RIAA Case."

Napster[8]

In 1999, I was in high school, cruising around in my car with a CD case that held around 100 CDs. That case held my entire music collection, which I acquired through purchases and gifts. The only places I could buy music were at shows, my local record store (Echos in Williamsburg, VA), or through Columbia House (a service that sent you free CDs each month for signing up). Gifting was a key part of album acquisition for me. My first two CDs were gifts from my sister. First, she gave me the Red Hot Chili Peppers' *Blood Sugar Sex Magik* when she got bored with it. I'm not quite sure how she got bored with it; I still listen to it regularly to this day. Second, for my birthday in 1995, she gave me Alanis Morrisette's *Jagged Little Pill* as my first new CD. As a 16-year-old, I was proud of my music collection—but longed for more music.

At the time, finding music on the Internet was laborious and ineffective. Internet radio provided low-quality access to music but contained the pitfalls of all radio in its lack of choice. MP3.com was a great site that allowed users to buy independent music. With your purchase, you could download mp3s and they would ship CDs with mp3s to you. In my opinion, MP3.com provided radical potential in its circumvention of major labels and its ability to provide alternative distribution, but it was limited in options. To this day, I still have some albums purchased through MP3.com in my music rotation. However, finding what you wanted online and downloading at an adequate speed was a challenge in the late 1990s.

A little later, in 1999, a friend told me about Napster (founded on June 1, 1999). This easy-to-use software application opened the world of music to me. Using peer-to-peer (p2p) networking, Napster allowed users to search for files on anyone's computer (in their shared folder) connected to the network. People could share most types of files, but the most popular were mp3s.[9] All of a sudden, the world of music was available with a few clicks of a mouse, from independent artists to major artists and new music to old music. Where record stores contained limited catalogs of music, Napster felt limitless.

But Napster's importance goes far beyond the distribution of music. Shawn Fanning, a student at Northeastern University at the time,[10] founded Napster by expanding on internet relay chat (IRC) technology to facilitate the transfer of files. Napster became the first p2p file-sharing technology to be available widely. By facilitating the transfer of files on a free platform, Napster and

---

8 Parts of this section were first published in Arditi, "Introduction."
9 Garofalo, "I Want My MP3: Who Owns Internet Music?"; McCourt and Burkart, "When Creators, Corporations and Consumers Collide"; Sterne, *MP3*.
10 Breen, "Napster 'Freedom' at Northeastern University."

Fanning embodied the Internet ethos where "information wants to be free."[11] It was this ethos described by Richard Barbrook and Andy Cameron as the "Californian ideology,"[12] an ideology that was never put into action as the free Internet became a giant shopping mall funded by venture capital investors at the turn of the century.

Napster made everyone take account of the idea that, yes, information can be free. However, the RIAA, major record labels, and Metallica,[13] among others, fought Napster and, later, every p2p file-sharing platform developed. They filed lawsuits against file-sharing services, and when that wasn't sufficient, they sued music fans. In 2007, I wrote my master's thesis contending that what the RIAA did was criminalize independent music.[14] According to the data I found, there was as much concern among the RIAA and major record labels that music fans could find music online that was not controlled by the major labels. File-sharing meant sharing one's own music as much as it meant someone else's music. Independent artists could not distribute music to record stores across the country, so uploading their music online presented a new opportunity for them to distribute music free. This means that not only was major label music available on Napster, but also music by potential competitors. By claiming p2p software only broke copyright law, the RIAA effectively criminalized those who chose to distribute their music there.

Reflecting on Napster a quarter century after its founding, one thing is clear: it changed the way we listen to music. In the digital vacuum left behind by the closure of p2p services rose new commercial ventures to distribute music online. First, the RIAA pushed music fans to download music from iTunes.[15] This was a change in mediation[16] that led to the "celestial jukebox"[17]—the idea that all music could be available online. Music went from $15 CDs to free downloads to $0.99 downloads. Second, the music industry coalesced behind a subscription model. With subscriptions, music consumption becomes constant and consistent in what I call "unending

---

11 Ashworth, "The Whole of the 'Whole Earth Catalog' Is Now Online"; Levy, "Hackers at 30."
12 Barbrook and Cameron, "The Californian Ideology."
13 Szrot, "Independent Music after Metallica v. Napster, Inc."; Patch, "Metallica, Napster and the Transformation of Subcultural Capital."
14 Arditi, *Criminalizing Independent Music: The Recording Industry Association of America's Advancement of Dominant Ideology.*
15 Arditi, "The State of Music"; Arditi, "iTunes"; Arditi, *iTake-Over.*
16 Mueller, "Napster's Mediations."
17 Burkart, "Music in the Cloud and the Digital Sublime"; Burkart and McCourt, *Digital Music Wars.*

consumption."[18] For example, the average music consumer spent $45 per year most years, even when the music industry was supposedly in decline.[19] But the subscription model means subscribers now pay about $120 per year for access to music,[20] a 300% increase, which doesn't include the revenue generated from the sale of records in the so-called vinyl revival.[21] The seductive drive to subscriptions stemmed from the celestial jukebox's solution to scarcity[22] by appearing to make all music available for a fee. Coincidentally, Dr. Dre sued Napster,[23] alongside Metallica, only to go on to develop Beats Music, a streaming company that would later become Apple Music (discussed in Chapter 4).[24]

In *A&M Records, Inc. v Napster, Inc.*, major record labels won by forcing the closure of Napster's p2p file-sharing platform.[25] A&M Records and the other complainants won because of an errant email where one of Napster's founders mentioned the platform would profit from users sharing music. For the courts, this was a clear instance of sharing music for commercial purposes—i.e., a copyright violation. According to the IFPI, it "is illegal to offer copyrighted material without permission of the rights holders and it is, therefore, just as illegal to build a commercial business on the basis of copyright infringement."[26] With Napster out of the way, the recording industry thought they could move beyond file-sharing. But Napster would not be the last p2p platform as KaZaA, Morpheus, Grokster, and a string of bit-torrents followed. Many of these platforms were outlawed because of their capacity to violate copyright law. When the iTunes store launched in 2003, the RIAA started suing individuals to encourage them to purchase $0.99 downloads—as I've argued elsewhere, the timing of these lawsuits lined up perfectly with the launch of iTunes.[27] The IFPI was candid about their strategy in the 2005 *Recording Industry in Numbers* report where it states:

---

18 Arditi, *Streaming Culture*; Arditi, "Digital Subscriptions."
19 Arditi, *iTake-Over*.
20 Arditi, "Digital Subscriptions."
21 Aswad, "Vinyl Sales Soar — and Even CDs Rebound — as U.S. Recorded Music Industry Posts $15 Billion Year-End Revenue"; Palm, "The New Old: Vinyl Records after the Internet"; Leight, "Vinyl Is Poised to Outsell CDs For the First Time Since 1986"; Skrimsjö, "Standing in the Way of Control."
22 Behrendtz, "Convenience Begets Capitalism"; Knowles, "The Artificiality of Digital Scarcity."
23 Kane, "Dr. Dre Sues Napster -- and Users?"
24 Arditi, "Digital Subscriptions."
25 Patel, A&M Records, Inc. v. Napster, Inc.; Scharf, "Napster's Long Shadow."
26 IFPI, "Recording Industry in Numbers," 2001, 3.
27 Arditi, "iTunes"; Arditi, *iTake-Over*.

"Lawsuits against individual file-sharers have changed attitudes, begun to reduce file-sharing in some countries, and stimulated legitimate services."[28] Their strategy was to offer iTunes as a "legitimate" alternative to file-sharing. This was the moment when the RIAA infamously sued their consumers both young and old. However, since their lawsuits were so large, these court cases were settled out of court rather than test their legality, so we have no concrete answer as to whether file-sharing violates copyright law.

The recording industry trade associations were candid about their goals in their reports.[29] "As long as internet pirate sites continue to thrive," the IFPI stated, "the development of the legitimate business will be seriously hampered."[30] Creating a *legitimate* platform was their explicit goal. "In order to create space for a legitimate internet business to develop, IFPI and its affiliated national groups across the world will continue to aggressively fight internet piracy. This is done through continuous monitoring of infringers, cooperation with ISPs and, where necessary, taking legal action."[31] Here the IFPI is clear that they support a digital platform where music fans can download music for a fee. The year after the report cited, Apple launched the iTunes store and lawsuits against individuals commenced.[32] But where do people go to download free music?

Closing the original Napster stalled the development of new file-sharing platforms, but it also stifled the creation of new technologies. New scientific discoveries and technologies build from previous scientific and technological developments. When technologies become locked down and controlled by corporations, it limits future creations.[33] The architecture of Napster allowed others to tinker with it, which means more people using Napster fostered new ideas that could one day reimagine the way we use the Internet.[34] Corporate oligopolies tend to limit new technologies because they protect intellectual property rights at the expense of the public.

However, the most consequential aspect of Napster was the way it enabled independent artists to share their music with other people. This was the threat to the music industry: fans being able to listen to music by independent artists

---

28 IFPI, "Recording Industry in Numbers," 2005, 3.
29 Arditi, "The Recording Industry in Numbers: A Record Label Centered View of Recorded Music"; Arditi, "The Global Music Report: Selling a Narrative of Decline."
30 IFPI, "Recording Industry in Numbers," 2002, 3.
31 Ibid., 3.
32 Arditi, *iTake-Over*.
33 Benkler, *The Wealth of Networks: How Social Production Transforms Markets and Freedom*; Gillespie, *Wired Shut: Copyright and the Shape of Digital Culture*.
34 Cornelius-Bell, "A Capitalist Stranglehold on 'Artificial Intelligence.'"

instead of major label artists. In a shared folder, there were no restrictions on what could be shared. I could share my writing alongside music I recorded of my independent artist friend and *Blood Sugar Sex Magik*. As someone searched for the Red Hot Chili Peppers, they may see my friend's music and listen to it. This act of listening to an independent artist comes into direct competition with other recording artists. Ultimately, this person may decide to see the independent artist in concert over the major label artist.

When music is available on the Internet, it makes it easier to find both major label and independent artists. Patryk Galuszka describes it as the "dilemma of democratization," a term he borrows from Brian Hracs, Doreen Jakob, and Atle Hauge,[35] where "the Internet makes it less costly to promote and distribute music to wide audiences; however, it simultaneously increases competition for access to listeners' ears, as more people try to succeed in the music business."[36] Whereas tape cassettes and CDs permitted small communities to circulate music over limited geographic distances, Napster allowed global distribution. Every person who posted music had the opportunity to spread music right alongside major label artists. Music was no longer scarce, but it became difficult to find music.

Napster appeared to solve the problem of scarcity for music[37] by establishing a mechanism for all people to share all their music. In the end, this would mean less money for labels, but labels wanted people to feel bad for recording artists. To do so, they deployed the piracy panic narrative to discourage music listeners from using file-sharing services.

Musicians

> Don't take away money from artists just like me
> How else can I afford another solid gold Humvee?
> And diamond studded swimming pools, these things don't grow on trees (Weird Al, "Don't Download This Song")[38]

When the RIAA propagated the piracy panic narrative, they did so in the defense of musicians. The former CEO of the RIAA, Hilary Rosen, stated the strategy simply, downloading "also hurts the very artists and songwriters

---

35 Hracs, Jakob, and Hauge, "Standing Out in the Crowd: The Rise of Exclusivity-Based Strategies to Compete in the Contemporary Marketplace for Music and Fashion."
36 Galuszka, "Showcase Festivals as a Gateway to Foreign Markets," 56.
37 Knowles, "The Artificiality of Digital Scarcity."
38 Yankovic, *Don't Download This Song*.

most downloaders profess to love."[39] While Rosen emphasizes the musicians, their only concern was recording industry revenue. The piracy panic narrative wouldn't work if they said, "don't download music because it hurts corporate profits." Record executives recognize the bond people have with their favorite recording artists. However, Weird Al cuts through the rhetoric by showing the irony that the biggest stars don't need our money. Who needs a diamond studded swimming pool? On the other hand, most recording artists never earn any money from recording music because record labels don't pay them for their work. Industry rhetoric about helping musicians during the file-sharing period obscures the fact record labels exploit musicians.

In 2002, there was a strategy funded by the major record labels and their trade associations where popular musicians appeared in advertisements on behalf of advocacy groups.[40] Britney Spears wrote "Would you go into a CD store and steal a CD? It's the same thing, people going into the computers and logging on and stealing our music."[41] Others participating in the campaign included Stevie Wonder, Luciano Pavarotti, Eminem, the Chicks (formerly the Dixie Chicks), and Beach Boy Brian Wilson, all published full-page newspaper ads across the United States. Meanwhile, each of these recognizable stars made a fortune from selling music—a hard group to empathize with for the average American. The RIAA's position was: you love musicians, why would you want to steal from them? Ironically, the public campaign in support of musicians was not discussed in the IFPI's yearly report, *Recording Industry in Numbers*, through this era.[42] In fact, musicians were not the concern of major record labels in their internal reflections on the industry, nor have they ever been a concern.

Compensation for musicians' labor is a real problem, which is a result of label exploitation. Musicians give up their rights to their work in exchange for a record contract—they sign away their masters (i.e., master recordings) to the label.[43] As a signed recording artist, musicians have no labor rights because they are classified as "independent contractors."[44] Contract law supersedes labor law in these instances. In the United States, record contracts mean that record labels are not responsible for minimum wage, Family and Medical

---

39 Ahrens, "Stars Come Out Against Net Music Piracy in New Ads."
40 Ibid.
41 Ibid.
42 Arditi, "The Recording Industry in Numbers: A Record Label Centered View of Recorded Music."
43 Osborne, *Owning the Masters*; Osborne, "Masters and Slaves: Black Artists and the Ownership of Sound Recording Copyright."
44 Arditi, "Record Contracts."

Leave, a 40-hour work week or overtime, equal employment, and employee provided health care because legally recording artists aren't their employees. On the other hand, everyone at the label who doesn't make music from janitorial staff to the executive suites are classified as employees.[45] However, musicians are the ones who create the labels' commodities: recorded music.

Record contracts give musicians an advance and potential access to the label's marketing departments and distribution networks in exchange for the master recordings of their music. Musical copyright has two main elements: (1) the copyright for the musical work, which protects the underlying composition and lyrics of a song; and (2) the copyright for the sound recording, which protects the individual performance (usually a recording) of a song.[46] A master recording[47] contains the copyright of the recording, and it is the recordings duplicated for distribution and performance. Recording artists usually retain their publishing rights for the musical works they compose/write, while giving up their master recording to their label. Other deals provide different scopes in the contract—for instance, 360 deals cover "360 degrees" of an artist's revenue potentially including performance rights, publishing rights, name-image-and-likeness, touring, and merchandise. Every contract is different, but the general terms apply.

An advance is an upfront payment on the potential sales of an artist's music. To state this in simple terms, I will use the example of CDs when they were at their apex in the 1990s.[48] An artist could get a $500,000 advance. With that advance, artists would record their album and pay themselves a stipend (usually around $20,000), this small stipend is the total pay the artist would receive over two years. Before an artist earns any revenue from the sale of their recordings, they must recoup (i.e., payback) the advance on their percentage of the royalties. A typical artist receives roughly 8–15% of the sale after retail is deducted. If we assume a 10% royalty, the math is easy. For the sale of a $15 CD, $5 comes off the top for the retailer. Royalties are calculated on the remaining $10. A recording artist then receives $1 royalty from the sale of every CD, but only after they recoup the advance. An album with a $500,000 advance recoups at the sale of 500,000 albums. A 500,000-selling album in the United States is an RIAA gold certified record. Very few artists ever have a gold selling album,[49] so under this equation, very few artists ever

---

45 Arditi, *Getting Signed*.
46 Klein, Moss, and Edwards, *Understanding Copyright*.
47 Osborne, *Owning the Masters*; Osborne, "Masters and Slaves: Black Artists and the Ownership of Sound Recording Copyright."
48 Arditi, "Record Contracts."
49 Osborne, "The Gold Disc: One Million Pop Fans Can't Be Wrong."

recoup their advance. If an artist sells 500,001 albums, they earn $1. At the same time, record labels earn roughly the same royalty on the sale of every album. The label breaks even at 250,000 units sold because they earn their 10% royalty plus the artist's 10% royalty (250,000 × 2 = 500,000). At the point when an album sells 500,000 units, the record label earns $250,000 while the artist earns $0! The system is far more complicated today, but the numbers work out to the same equation.

All of this is to say, most musicians earn very little, if anything, from the sale of albums because of the terms set by record labels. Yet when the RIAA filed lawsuits against individuals for file-sharing, they claimed damages at the greatest extent of the law by claiming file-sharing hurt recording artists—$150,000 per song.[50] Before the RIAA filed these lawsuits, Metallica sued Napster users for $100,000 per song. In a massive show of force, Lars Ulrich, Metallica's drummer, provided 300,000 names of people who shared Metallica's music in the previous 24 hours.[51] In other words, Ulrich and Metallica claimed they were harmed for $30 *billion* in 24 hours, far exceeding their total record sales at the time. Damages of either $100,000 or $150,000 per song is outlandish. How can a song be worth $150,000 per download if most songs never come close to generating that much revenue? Very few artists ever make that amount total for a song, nonetheless per person. This reflects the position that music's availability online is a commercial copyright violation—the uploader has a far larger reach than themselves, they commercially distribute the music. However, no reasonable person would agree Metallica, or any musician could suffer a $30 billion loss in one day.

The RIAA and major record labels based their data on loss of income for musicians on projections about reduced CD sales. In the next section, I demonstrate why CD sales dropped. Instead of being caused by rampant music piracy, the problem is a murky result of a confluence of factors.

Why Did CD Sales Fall?

At the turn of the twenty-first century, CD sales dropped. As Figure 2.1 in Chapter 2 shows, each new mediation prior to the mp3 resulted in an increase in overall sales. When CD sales dropped, there was no new viable format to purchase music until the launch of the iTunes Store in 2003.[52] Plummeting CD sales worried major record labels, a corporate oligarchy that felt entitled

---

50 Blau, "Music Biz Sues Student File-Swappers."
51 Patch, "Metallica, Napster and the Transformation of Subcultural Capital."
52 Arditi, "iTunes."

to consumer cash. Based on CD sales, record labels had reason to panic as their key commodity lost revenue, but the overall picture of music appeared vibrant—mp3 players allowed new levels of portability, digital audio workstations (DAWs) made home recording cheap and accessible, CD-RW drives allowed musicians to distribute their own music, and a booming independent music scene added to the diversity of music. While CD sales fell, the problem for major record labels materialized from the loss of the album-replacement cycle and competition from other sources of entertainment.

The idea of a CD sales plummet following the release of Napster is patently false. Figure 3.1 shows the RIAA reports on CD shipments versus recorded sales by Nielsen SoundScan. Shipments count the number of units shipped to a record store. These are not the same as sales. If a record store does not sell a unit, it ships it back to the label, but that does not get subtracted from the RIAA's reporting on shipments. On the other hand, Nielsen SoundScan reports actual sales using point-of-sales data. You can see the difference between the RIAA and Nielsen in Figure 3.1 where a leveling begins to occur in 2000.[53] This leveling occurred with the rise of just-in-time

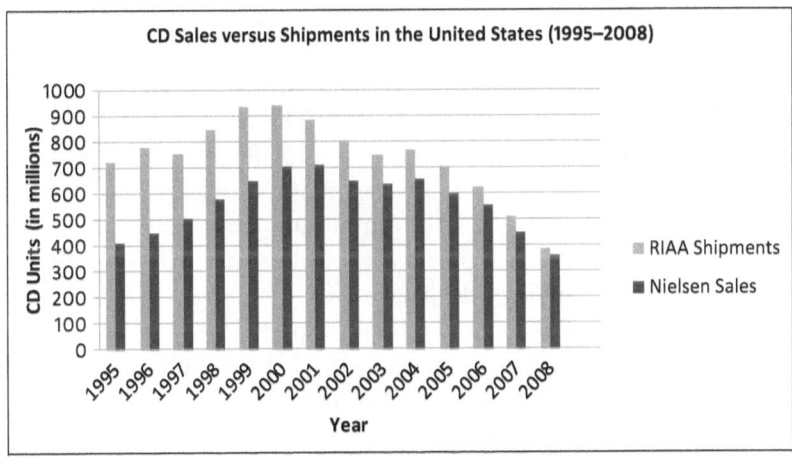

Figure 3.1 CD Sales versus Shipments in the United States (1995–2008).

---

53 "SoundScan 1996 Year-End Music Industry Report"; "SoundScan 1998 Year-End Music Industry Report"; "SoundScan 2000 Year-End Music Industry Report"; "SoundScan 2002 Year-End Music Industry Report"; "SoundScan 2004 Year-End Music Industry Report"; "SoundScan 2006 Year-End Music Industry Report"; "SoundScan 2010 Year-End Music Industry Report"; IFPI, "Recording Industry in Numbers," 2001; IFPI, "Recording Industry in Numbers," 2011.

production. Just-in-time production is a global supply chain that cuts back on overproduction of commodities because retailers can carry smaller supplies and quickly reorder when there is demand.[54] According to Nielsen, CD sales increased in 1999, 2000, and 2001, dropping for the first time in 2002, whereas the RIAA reported slower growth in 2000 and decreases in CD shipments beginning in 2001. These are important data points because they show the piracy panic narrative is based on a problematic argument.

When the IFPI communicates with itself in its yearly report, the *Recording Industry in Numbers* (*RIN*), the trade organization is candid about the causes of the condition of the industry.[55] The 2002 *RIN* states "the recent fall in CD sales to a maturation of the 'CD-replacement cycle' in the largest markets, whereby consumers have repurchased albums on CD that they had previously bought on cassette or LP."[56] As discussed in Chapter 2, the real loss for the industry comes from a reduction in catalog sales. Since anyone with a CD-ROM drive could rip their music catalog onto their computers, there was no reason for people to repurchase their collected music. The album-replacement cycle allows record labels to generate revenue from catalog music sales, but there was no reason to do so with mp3s. iTunes recreated the album replacement cycle for major record labels. According to the *RIN*,[57] following the launch of the iTunes Store in 2003, singles skyrocketed (see Figure 3.2). While part of this rise came from new music releases, catalog sales played a major part in the growth of digital singles. This is most clearly evidenced by the release of The Beatles' catalog on iTunes. For years, The Beatles resisted releasing their catalog on the iTunes Store. After they finally released their catalog in November 2010, sales of The Beatles' music increased rapidly selling 2 million songs and 450,000 albums.[58] Mp3s made purchasing catalog music in new mediations obsolete, but the iTunes Store and marketing reinvigorated those sales, especially among older generations.

The IFPI also shared a concern that competition with other forms of popular culture led to declines in music sales. The 2003 *RIN* stated: "Sales have been affected by competition from newer forms of entertainment,

---

54 Smith, "Tommy Hilfiger in the Age of Mass Customization"; LaFeber, *Michael Jordan and the New Global Capitalism*.
55 Arditi, "The Global Music Report: Selling a Narrative of Decline."
56 IFPI, "Recording Industry in Numbers," 2002, 8.
57 IFPI, "Recording Industry in Numbers," 2001; IFPI, "Recording Industry in Numbers," 2008.
58 Serjeant, "Beatles Sell over 2 Million in First Week on iTunes"; Ogg, "The Beatles Come to iTunes at Last"; Bruno, "Beatles Catalog Finally Coming to iTunes, Apple Announces."

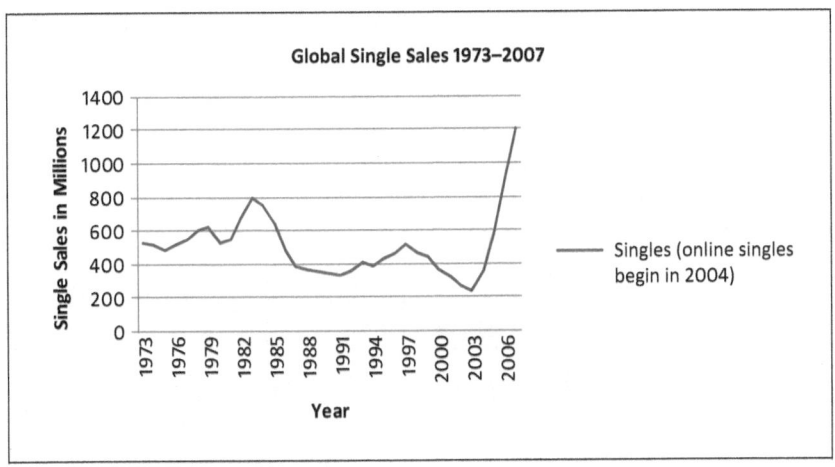

Figure 3.2 Global single sales.

particularly DVD and video games which saw strong growth in 2002. This has reduced the amount of retail space available to CDs and cut into consumer spending on music."[59] A year later, the IFPI coined the term "lifestyle music" to show how interconnected music is with other forms of popular culture. They determined "though these sectors continue to compete for 'share of wallet', music is a key component in the finished products or services offered in each of these segments—something music companies have been successfully exploiting in terms of strategic licensing."[60] In other words, if you can't beat them, join them. Ultimately, this strategy led to the licensing schemes in hit games like *Guitar Hero*, *Rock Band*, and *Grand Theft Auto V*.[61]

While the RIAA, IFPI, and major record labels publicly blamed file-sharing for declines in CD sales, they privately knew their business model was outdated. The piracy panic narrative told a story of fans killing music by downloading music. They did so by asking fans to care about their favorite

---

59 IFPI, "Recording Industry in Numbers," 2003.
60 IFPI, "Recording Industry in Numbers," 2004, 17.
61 Pham, "The Return of Guitar Hero and Rock Band: Comeback or Throwback?"; Ambrosino, "Aerosmith Made More Money from 'Guitar Hero' than from Any One of Its Albums"; Arditi, "Synergy and Syncs"; Arditi, "Video Game Concerts"; Arditi, "Music Everywhere"; Dozal, "Consumerism Hero: The 'Selling Out' of Guitar Hero and Rock Band."

musicians. But by arguing fans were hurting their favorite musicians, the industry ignored the fact musician exploitation is a product of recording industry practices. This created an atmosphere where music fans became the enemy, and those fans were scared to participate in perfectly legal practices like ripping music and burning CDs. Many people changed their practices because they didn't want to be pirates, and yet, the recording industry continued to stoke a narrative to force fans to comply with their preferred methods of music consumption.

Chapter 4

STREAMING: USER-GENERATED VIDEO IS KILLING MUSIC

In a 2007 video, a baby who was not old enough to walk pushes a Fisher Price walker. As he shuffles by his mom, she asks "what do you think of the music?" At this point, if you listen hard, you can tell the barely audible distorted music is Prince's "Let's Go Crazy." The baby starts bopping up and down. After eight months, only 28 people viewed the video, mainly friends and family, but Universal Music asked YouTube to take down the video.[1] YouTube complied, but that was only the beginning of the saga.

Following the takedown, Stephanie Lenz (the mother) filed a lawsuit against Universal with the help of the Electronic Frontier Foundation (EFF). Ultimately, federal courts ruled in favor of Lenz.[2] The judiciary found the video was protected by fair use. While YouTube is a commercial website, Lenz did not post it for commercial purposes, but rather to share a cute moment with family. Lenz and EFF argued that no one would seriously think the video was a way to subvert copyright law.[3] In the court's ruling, "presiding judge Richard Tallman wrote that 'fair use is not just excused by the law, it is wholly authorized by the law' — so it has to be part of a copyright holder's legal considerations."[4] Universal Music Group made the motion because they felt it would be onerous to determine if every instance of an uploaded song was fair use or not, but the court was not moved by their argument.

The dancing baby story is a fascinating story considering Prince's place in the music industry. Prince infamously took on his record label. First, he performed with "slave" written on his cheek because he argued the conditions

---

1 "The Home Video Prince Doesn't Want You to See."
2 Thanawala, "YouTube Video of Baby Dancing to Prince Track Sparks Trial over Copyright."
3 Cornish, Lenz, and Nazer, "Appeals Court Rules Youtube Video Of Baby Dancing To Prince Was Fair Use."
4 Robertson, "'Dancing Baby' Ruling Says Fair Use Matters in Copyright Takedowns."

of his record contracts enslaved him to the record company.[5] He stated, "If you don't own your masters, your master owns you."[6] Then he broke free of that relationship by painstakingly changing his name to a symbol. This transgressive artist, who resisted record label dominance, sold out to Universal, which wanted to punish a family for showing a kid dancing to Prince's music.

More importantly, the episode demonstrates the new battle lines between the music industry and the public in the streaming era.[7] Before recording technology, a musical performance was clear cut: a person playing music in front of another person. Recording technology and radio shifted the question of performance to a technically engineered form of performance. But with streaming technology, what counts as a performance or a sale? How much is a performance worth? Who pays and how much? These questions become even more complex as the recording industry attempts to delegitimize any form of music listening or usage that it does not approve first.

Piracy Dies, But Long Live the Piracy Panic Narrative

While the Prince vs. dancing baby episode played out during the zenith of the RIAA's battle against file-sharing pirates, the lawsuit signaled changes to come as downloading became less popular with the rise of music streaming platforms (MSPs). In the streaming era, piracy dies.[8] As piracy shifted from tapes to CDs; CDs to Napster; Napster to KaZaA; KaZaA to bit-torrents, the major record labels promoted the piracy panic narrative to stifle innovation, community, and culture. When Spotify, YouTube, and Apple Music became more popular, piracy became irrelevant as the cost per stream is now close to zero or requires consuming an advertisement. People no longer need to pirate music because the celestial jukebox[9] made most music available online, usually for close to free. And yet, the transition to streaming did not stop the piracy panic narrative, but rather changed the folk devil to digital companies with Hollywood pitted against Silicon Valley.

---

5 Arditi, "Record Contracts"; Osborne, "Masters and Slaves: Black Artists and the Ownership of Sound Recording Copyright."
6 Pareles, "A Re-Inventor of His World and Himself – Document – Gale OneFile: Business."
7 Arditi, *iTake-Over*.
8 Streaming made file-sharing obsolete. This effectively kills piracy because the cost per stream is effectively zero. File-sharing usage has declined as a result. However, the RIAA, IFPI, and major record labels continue to claim piracy does damage to the recording industry.
9 Burkart and McCourt, *Digital Music Wars*.

In my book *Streaming Culture*, I define streaming as the following:

> To stream is to have constant motion, and constant change. Streaming is fleeting and always changing. If you think about a stream of water, the water is in motion. If you drop a leaf on top of a stream, the water carries it down stream quickly. The only constant is that the water moves past you. The stream is ever-changing, much like culture. Culture is streaming.[10]

Similar to live music, streaming music can only be experienced in the moment of the stream. A big difference between live music and streaming music stems from the fact live music exists in the ephemeral in a way that it only happens in the moment, but streaming music can be experienced in a moment repeatedly. As a result, a stream is difficult to attach monetary value to. The recording industry seemed to settle on the value of a downloaded song at $1 from the value of a CD—if a CD ranges from 12 to 16 songs, and a CD costs roughly $15, then each song is worth roughly $1. They settled on the $10 digital album because distribution and retail costs were reduced (a process known as disintermediation).[11] But how do you value something that is so fleeting?

MSPs pay labels a fraction of a penny for each stream. Streaming music services work on the aggregate where massive numbers of people stream music using subscriptions or via ad-support. If you have the world of music at your fingertips for $10 per month or free with an occasional advertisement, then there is no reason to download music. However, not every stream has the same value according to the industry. Recording industry insiders have focused on the amount artists earn per stream, but these numbers are highly misleading.[12] David Hesmondhalgh presents an analysis of the data and rhetoric around streaming renumeration that focuses on (1) the size of the revenue pot for MSPs, (2) the amount MSPs pay rights holders (i.e. labels), and (3) the amount rights holders pay musicians.[13] The payments themselves derive from a pro-rata system, which pays rights holders based on the total number streams.[14] This means artists earn more money based on the total percentage of overall streams they receive (not only on a per stream basis); therefore, top streamers

---

10 Arditi, *Streaming Culture*, 9.
11 Arditi, *iTake-Over*.
12 Hesmondhalgh, "Is Music Streaming Bad for Musicians?"
13 Ibid., 3599–3600.
14 For a detailed discussion about pro-rata renumeration please see Anderton and Hannam, "Pressing Reset."

earn more per stream than artists with fewer streams. Chris Anderton and James Hannam maintain record labels focus on per streams, "rather than on the deals and structures that record companies have negotiated with them, or on the pro rata (rather than per stream) accounting practices that are common to the sector."[15] This helps place the blame on MSPs and construct musicians as the victims, while the actual system depends on the mechanics of capitalism and the broader music industry.

From early in the digital era, labels made clear that not every stream has the same value. During the analog era, AM/FM radio never had performance rights for the sound recording of a song, so a radio station pays a performance royalty for the musical work, not the recorded song. In other words, when a DJ plays a song on terrestrial (AM/FM) radio, the station pays royalties to the songwriter, but not the recording artist. This is something that has always irked the major labels and was a holdover from when radio stations were the dominant players in the broader music industry.[16] After heavy lobbying from the recording industry, former-president Bill Clinton signed the Digital Performance Right in Sound Recordings Act (DPRA) in 1995 to change this rule. The DPRA created a performance right for digital transmissions while providing exemptions for terrestrial radio—i.e., radio stations would not have to pay royalties for the sound recording. Furthermore, the law distinguishes two types of digital transmissions: noninteractive and interactive. For noninteractive streams, users do not have the ability to pick songs they hear—similar to traditional radio, like SiriusXM satellite radio and Pandora internet radio. The DPRA permitted automatic licenses for all music at a set (relatively low) royalty rate. On the other hand, the DPRA required interactive transmissions to receive licenses from copyright owners, and they had to negotiate royalty rates. Most music on Spotify and Apple Music are examples of interactive transmissions where users choose the music they hear. This is why there are frequently stories about artists not including their music on Spotify or Apple Music, but not for SiriusXM or Pandora. However, major record labels favor Spotify and Apple Music because they can produce higher returns with their negotiated licenses.

The music industry's emphasis on revenue demonstrates that music listening only counts when it produces value. Specifically, the recording industry only counts listening practices when fans consume music. Consumption inherently links listening practices to capitalism. When people "consume" music, they generate revenue for the music industry whether they buy a CD, subscribe to

---

15 Ibid., 50.
16 Litman, *Digital Copyright*.

Spotify, watch ads on YouTube, or purchase a concert ticket. The *Billboard* charts only track revenue-generating music listens. This creates a system dependent on democratic consumption.

Democratic consumption is the idea that people vote with their wallets. According to those who evaluate culture through democratic consumption, the best way to measure the popularity of a cultural good is by measuring what earns the most money. Theodor Adorno and Max Horkheimer criticize this approach by stating the "industry bows to the vote it has itself rigged."[17] Because record labels spend an absurd amount of money on marketing music, they ensure people purchase the music they produce. However, this also misses a lot of listening practices that would give a broader sense of a song's popularity. Radio has always been difficult to track listens, and like other forms of advertising driven sources, the market for radio depends on the type of goods they can advertise, catering more toward audiences with expendable income.[18] During the tape cassette and CD eras, the recording industry didn't care what people listened to, they cared what people purchased. This meant that the music on mixtapes didn't count toward chart data.[19] Again, in the downloading era, the recording industry made no attempts to quantify music downloads from file-sharing websites to measure popularity while they did use services like BigChampagne to use the data to decide where to send artists on tour.[20] What counts is what sells. But it is also important to remember that what sells is usually the most marketed music. Record labels have an incentive to heavily promote some of their music because the better a song or album performs on the charts, the more it will sell in the long run. Democratic consumption becomes the way to measure the investment major record labels put into promoting their own music.

The practice of counting consumption over listening (i.e., democratic consumption) continues in the streaming era. Each streaming platform operates differently. Most MSPs rely on demand economies of scale, which means that the presence of more users makes the platform more valuable to

---

17 Horkheimer and Adorno, "The Culture Industry: Enlightenment as Mass Deception."
18 Jhally, *The Codes of Advertising: Fetishism and the Political Economy of Meaning in the Consumer Society*; Baker, *Media, Markets, and Democracy*; Smythe, "On the Audience Commodity and Its Work"; Fuchs, "Dallas Smythe Today – The Audience Commodity, the Digital Labour Debate, Marxist Political Economy and Critical Theory. Prolegomena to a Digital Labour Theory of Value."
19 Drew, *Unspooled*; Harrison, "'Cheaper than a CD, plus We Really Mean It': Bay Area Underground Hip Hop Tapes as Subcultural Artifacts"; Burns, *Mixtape Nostalgia*.
20 Arditi, "Disciplining the Consumer: File-Sharers under the Watchful Eye of the Music Industry."

both record labels and users.[21] However, the patchwork of architectures and laws that support MSPs means major record labels have varying degrees of support for different platforms from high support for Spotify and Apple Music to indifference for Bandcamp. Streams and downloads only count when the platform monetizes music. Music fans with money who subscribe to platform count more than free or ad-supported services. Billboard counts YouTube, SoundCloud, and Spotify ad-supported streams less on its charts because they have less monetary value per stream. The rest of this section describes YouTube, Spotify, Apple Music, Pandora, and Bandcamp as streaming platforms that changed the way the music industry operates.

Pandora

The 1990s saw a variety of attempts at internet radio, but few of them caught on. Radio is not only a part of the music industry, but it was also the dominant way to listen to music through the 1940s. Even to this day, radio is popular and powerful. However, listeners are always limited by what AM/FM radio waves are available in any local market. Internet radio became popular with the idea that an internet radio station could provide broader access to a variety of music. This was especially true given the radio consolidation that occurred following the passage of the Telecommunications Act of 1996.[22] Today, iHeartMedia (formerly Clear Channel Communications) owns over 855 radio stations across the United States.[23] This creates homogeneous music available to listeners across the United States because iHeartMedia creates the same channel to broadcast across the country with local tie-ins. Internet radio provided the potential for more options, but didn't provide effective options until the launch of Pandora Radio.

In 2000, Will Glaser, John Craft, and Tim Westergren founded Pandora Radio, an internet radio station that fed users music to their taste, the platform became widely available in 2005. Pandora used what its founders called the "music genome," a massive musicological undertaking to categorize music based on specific traits, which they call "genes." "Genes could include," Robert Prey lists, "the gender of the lead vocalist, the tempo of the chorus, the level of distortion on the electric guitar, the type of background vocals, and many more."[24] Different genres have a different number of genes attributable

---

21 Leyshon and Watson, *The Rise of the Platform Music Industries*, 5.
22 McChesney, *The Problem of the Media: U.S. Communication Politics in the Twenty-First Century*; Baker, *Media Concentration and Democracy: Why Ownership Matters*.
23 Sisario and Merced, "The Radio Giant iHeartMedia Prepares for Possible I.P.O."
24 Prey, "Nothing Personal."

to them, but the genes work outside of genres as well. As people listen to Pandora they can provide feedback with a thumbs up or thumbs down. This feedback refines the algorithm and changes the characteristics of the station. Tim Anderson claims the "genius of the service is that it allows users to create a stream that is customized to their tastes with relative ease based on a combination of proprietary and user-generated data points."[25] The more people listen, the more entuned the list is to the user.

YouTube[26]

When YouTube launched in 2005, it was the first website to make it easy for users to upload user-generated multimedia content. Suddenly, anyone with a high-speed internet connection could post videos online. This made major record labels nervous because they feared users could upload their music and they would be unable to stop unlicensed uploading. As part of the Digital Millennium Copyright Act (DMCA), websites were given safe harbor, which means they would not be liable for unlicensed or illegal content they had uploaded on their websites.[27] These rules "exempt online intermediaries from liability for materials hosted by their systems."[28] However, the limitation was that sites could only have safe harbor if they agreed to remove illegal content following a takedown notice. This is what created the controversy around the baby dancing to Prince's music (discussed above).

Importantly, YouTube changed how people access music. YouTube enabled people to search for a song and stream it. It brought users closer to the "celestial jukebox."[29] Whereas file-sharing websites, and even the iTunes Store, required people to download music, YouTube permitted streaming. The platform accelerated the shift from music ownership to access.[30] Users began to find it easier to listen to music through streams than downloading them. But the rise of YouTube as an MSP led to moral panics. Jean Burgess and Joshua Green observed, "in media coverage of YouTube, stories exhibiting the moral panic draw on and amplify two interlocking strains of

---

25 Anderson, *Popular Music in a Digital Music Economy*, 98.
26 This section is about YouTube, not YouTube Music. YouTube Music is a subscription service launched in 2015. This MSP operates more like Spotify and Apple Music.
27 Copyright Alliance, "DMCA Safe Harbor | Copyright Alliance."
28 Leyshon and Watson, *The Rise of the Platform Music Industries*, 37.
29 Burkart and McCourt, *Digital Music Wars*.
30 Bennett, *Corporate Life in the Digital Music Industry*, 36.

public anxiety: youth and morality on the one hand, and new media and its 'effects' on the other."[31] Record labels stoked these anxieties to discourage music consumption on YouTube. Their reliance on moral panics made relying on YouTube's broad access to deep catalogs of music seem as if they were doing something wrong even though streaming music on YouTube is completely legal.

There is one big difference between YouTube and other MSPs because YouTube plays videos. This led *Billboard* to count streams on YouTube differently than other platforms (discussed more below). First, while the Billboard Hot 100 (the singles chart) counted YouTube streams in its formula to calculate the most popular singles, it did not count YouTube streams toward album totals on the Billboard 200. *Billboard* began counting YouTube streams for the Billboard 200 in January 2020, seven years after it began counting singles.[32] Second, all streams on YouTube count less than streams on Spotify and Apple Music. YouTube pays less per stream than other platforms because they argue there are more royalties to pay out with videos—they must pay the video director, producer, etc.[33] To ensure users watch the videos, YouTube has tried different tactics. For instance, YouTube began pausing videos when users switch tabs. This stops users from using YouTube as an MSP and encourages them to subscribe to YouTube Music if this is how they use it. Furthermore, when users watch ad-supported YouTube videos, they pay less due to the DPRA.

Many scholars have looked to YouTube as an example of participatory culture. But the examples of uploading videos to begin a music career from Justin Bieber to Okay Go "do not in themselves realize the myth of DIY celebrity so much as they demonstrate its limits."[34] What counts is what sells. The recording industry has a long history of undercounting music genres developed by Black artists, especially hip-hop.[35] Hip-hop fans transitioned from mixtapes to YouTube, which contributes to the way the recording industry undercounts hip-hop music. For instance, NBA YoungBoy is the top YouTube artist, but often lags behind on the *Billboard* charts because Nielsen SoundScan excludes many of the streams.[36] That means that not all listens are equal and artists who rely on YouTube suffer as a result.

---

31 Burgess and Green, *YouTube*, 18.
32 "Billboard 200 Makeover."
33 Holmes, "Artists Claim YouTube Pays Them Less Than Spotify. Are They Right?"
34 Burgess and Green, *YouTube*, 23.
35 Watkins, *Hip Hop Matters: Politics, Pop Culture, and the Struggle for the Soul of a Movement*.
36 Rolli, "The Billboard 200 Will Incorporate YouTube Streams In 2020."

Spotify

In 2006, Daniel Ek and Martin Lorentzon founded Spotify, an MSP that would change the way we listen to and interact with music. Based on a "freemium" business model, Spotify allows users to stream music via an ad-supported service or for a monthly subscription. A freemium model's goal is to entice free (i.e., ad-supported) users to subscribe. Like Pandora, people who use Spotify's ad-supported service have a limit on the number of tracks they can skip and they have to periodically listen to ads. However, a subscription allows users to listen to Spotify's entire catalog and skip as many tracks as they like. The goal was a "shift from ownership to access."[37] If people could give up on the idea of a record collection, they could access a massive catalog for a relatively low monthly charge. Spotify seemed to make the celestial jukebox a lived reality.

To garner a large user base, Spotify needed access to the major labels' music catalogs. At the time, record labels were concerned about whether they would profit to their liking from MSPs. As a result, Spotify gave major labels equity in the company in exchange for licenses to the major labels' music.[38] According to *Rolling Stone*, "Sony BMG (now Sony Music) got the biggest stake of at 6%; Universal Music Group got 5%; Warner Music Group got 4%; EMI Music got 2%; Merlin got 1%."[39] When Spotify began publicly trading its stock, the labels sold their equity in a variety of ways netting hundreds of millions of dollars; Universal Music Group still retains 3.27% equity in Spotify with a value of over $3 billion.[40] I highlight this to show that even though labels claim they are not profitable, they earn money from their investments in Spotify that they do not include in their revenue reports when they complain about the state of the music business.

Part of the deal that gave labels equity in Spotify in exchange for music licenses stipulated that Spotify could not distribute original music.[41] This stopped Spotify from becoming the Netflix of music. Netflix's streaming platform started as an a la carte service with access to a massive catalog

---

37 Eriksson et al., *Spotify Teardown*, 154.
38 Lesser, "Record Labels Shot the Artists, But They Did Not Share the Equity"; Ingham, "Here's Exactly How Many Shares the Major Labels and Merlin Bought in Spotify – and What Those Stakes Are Worth Now."
39 Ingham, "If Universal Music Sells Its Spotify Stock Right Now, Artists Get $500 Million."
40 Ingham, "Universal Music Group's Stock in Spotify Is Worth $3bn. Time to Sell?"
41 Karp, "Streaming Sidesteps The Labels."

of television shows and films, but in the 2010s, it began to produce its own content. The reason Spotify hasn't followed the Netflix model is because of the license agreements that gave labels equity. To upload music independent musicians must use a third party, like CD Baby, which clears all the copyright issues and acts as an intermediary for independent artists on Spotify (and other MSPs). In 2018, Spotify briefly sidestepped this agreement by signing non-exclusive deals with independent artists—these artists sign with Spotify only to have their music on Spotify while they can sign separate deals with other platforms.[42] Ultimately, Spotify gave up on permitting artists to register their own music on the platform.

Much has been written about the renumeration inequities artists face on Spotify, but the actual business strategies remain opaque—exemplified by the labels' equity-for-license scheme. This is standard practice under capitalism as "Media companies whose main outputs are defined as information goods protected by intellectual property standards understandably prefer secrecy over public scrutiny."[43] The recording industry is especially guarded about its data as record labels publicly complain about streaming's value without providing access to company data. Labels continually hide how the recording industry counts music revenue. In the pre-SoundScan era, *Billboard* counted music sales by asking how many albums or singles an artist sold. The system was rampant with corruption as label employees gave merchandise and tickets to record store clerks who labels knew would be polled. When SoundScan implemented a point-of-sale system, Billboard had a snapshot of actual sales. Now with MSPs, we can get an exact idea about market revenue. Spotify reported a record 268 million paid subscribers in 2025 at roughly $10 per month, that is on pace to bring in over $32 billion in subscription revenue alone, but they also reported over 600 million ad-supported users per month as well.[44] I highlight this because if the IFPI reported even a portion of the overall subscription revenue at Spotify to its industry data, it would show the recording industry as far more valuable than their reported data.[45]

---

42 Ibid.
43 Eriksson et al., *Spotify Teardown*, 181.
44 Huston, "Spotify Adds Record Number of Users in Quarter, Paid Subscribers Hit 268M."
45 Arditi, "The Global Music Report: Selling a Narrative of Decline."

Apple Music[46]

Apple changed the music industry in 2003 with the launch of the iTunes Store.[47] The deals Apple arranged with the major record labels to sell downloads for $0.99 per song or $9.99 per album changed the recording industry. But Apple itself became a dinosaur when it did not quickly transition to streaming. To reinvigorate its brand as a technology innovator with a popular culture edge, Apple had to look elsewhere for an MSP and ultimately, they purchased Beats Music. Beats Music was an MSP started by hip-hop mogul Dr. Dre and music industry executive Jimmy Iovine in 2012. Apple purchased Beats Electronics in 2014, but I argue elsewhere, the popular Beats headphones were the smallest part of the deal.[48] The subscription service was far more valuable as it gave Apple a streaming platform.

Unlike Spotify, Apple Music doesn't have a freemium option—the only way to listen to the service is to be a subscriber. In June 2024, Apple Music had 93 million subscribers. This represents a smaller, but significant, subscriber base than Spotify. Most importantly, Apple consumers love Apple. An expressed reason Apple purchased Beats Electronics was to hire Dr. Dre and Jimmy Iovine to replace some of the cultural capital lost with the death of Steve Jobs.[49] However, the hiring of Dr. Dre is also a reminder of the conflict over file-sharing as he was one of the plaintiffs who sued Napster (discussed in Chapter 3). Apple has a cultural pull that perpetuates its subscriber base and makes it appealing to major record labels.

Alternatives

Two alternatives to the dominant MSPs are worth noting, which provide producer-oriented music to the public.[50] First, Bandcamp is a music platform that offers independent music via streaming, downloads, and mail order physical CDs, vinyl, and tape cassettes, in addition to other merchandise. Bandcamp grew in popularity during the pandemic when it started Bandcamp Friday, a day where the company waves its fees to support independent music. Second,

---

46 For an extensive discussion and description of Apple Music's acquisition of Beats Electronics, please see Arditi, "Digital Subscriptions."
47 Arditi, "iTunes."
48 Arditi, "Digital Subscriptions."
49 Ibid.
50 Hesmondhalgh, Jones, and Rauh, "SoundCloud and Bandcamp as Alternative Music Platforms."

SoundCloud is a streaming platform for independent musicians to share music via streaming. SoundCloud has been especially important to the hip-hop community with a subgenre being coined "SoundCloud rap." In the context of democratic consumption, both SoundCloud and Bandcamp are in liminal positions in the broader music industry. Bandcamp's streams count toward *Billboard* charts because they are all "sales" in the classic sense, but free streams on the website do not count. SoundCloud streams only count toward *Billboard* charts when the artist decides to monetize.[51] As a result of the way *Billboard* calculates chart positions, it is clear the recording industry remains heavily involved in regulating consumption and distribution in the streaming era.

The Panic

> The value gap is about the gross mismatch between music being enjoyed by consumers and the revenues being returned to the music community. Today, music consumption is exploding, driven by streaming services and in particular by the rapidly-growing use of user upload platforms such as YouTube.—Frances Moore, CEO of IFPI[52]

With the above statement by Frances Moore, CEO of the IFPI, the global recording industry set its sights beyond piracy. Streaming music through licensed digital services is perfectly legal, but the recording industry still pressures consumers with their view of the proper ways to stream music. The IFPI settled on the "value gap" as the new folk devil in 2015.[53] In the first report on the value gap, they mention the perceived impact YouTube's safe harbor protection has on "creators and rights owners."[54] They slip creators in because they want music fans to empathize with the plight of recording artists, but the real focus is the impact on rights owners or holders (i.e., labels). "The sudden elevation of this supposed 'value gap' above the bugaboo of piracy is all the more surprising because term didn't even exist until about 2016," according to the Electronic Frontier Foundation, "when it was created out of whole cloth as a device to explain why copyright holders should be entitled to a larger slice of Internet platform revenues." By replacing piracy with the value gap, the recording industry hoped to stir the public again in the interests of artists.

---

51 Hampp, "SoundCloud Debuts Monetization Play With 'On SoundCloud', Announces $100 Million In Funding."
52 IFPI, "Global Music Report," 5.
53 IFPI, "Digital Music Report 2015."
54 Ibid.

The problem is the interests of the major record labels and their recording artists do not align. Labor creates all value according to the labor theory of value, an economic theory discussed by a diverse range of economists.[55] In Karl Marx's understanding of a value gap, the gap is the amount of value created by workers that they do not receive in their wages; he calls this surplus value.[56] For Marx, surplus value represents the gap between the use value of labor (i.e., the value labor produces) and the exchange value of labor (i.e., the wage paid to the laborer).[57] Instead of calling this surplus value, we can call it the rate of exploitation. The recording industry appropriates the idea of a value gap for their own designs. While the recording industry's "value gap" operates through the idea that some entity under values workers for their labor, their value gap is pure ideology—an upside-down vision of reality that expresses the ideas of the dominant class. By arguing MSPs underpay recording artists, the IFPI flips the exploitation of artists on its head. MSPs pay record labels and record labels pay artists—MSPs do not pay artists. Record labels create surplus value by refusing to pay recording artists the value they get through their production of recordings. Because of the recording industry's effective rhetoric, music fans feel as if MSPs do not effectively compensate recording artists. The industry's hope is that fans support legislative fixes developed by the recording industry, then they can profit from the added surplus value through increased revenue from MSPs.

As always, the recording industry claims to be very concerned about their artists' rights. "What if we're all watching the Grammys a few years from now," Neil Portnow then-president of the Recording Academy posited at the 2015 Grammys, "and there's no Best New Artist award because there aren't enough talented artists or songwriters who are actually able to make a living from their craft?"[58] The issue recording industry identified in the streaming era is that mainstream MSPs do not compensate artists fairly. This is the version of the "value gap" the recording industry brought forward at the Grammys in 2015. Portnow presented the theme of "killing music" because he states that there would be no new artists willing to work without earning money, which is patently false. First, this defies thousands of years of music production by human beings where there was no compensation. Second, plenty of people record music today and do not make a living from it or even have a desire to earn money. Finally, this is a problem of record labels not

---

55 Smith, *An Inquiry into the Nature and Causes of the Wealth of Nations*; Attali, *Noise: The Political Economy of Music*; Marx, *Capital*.
56 Marx, *Capital*.
57 Ibid.
58 "57th Annual Grammy Awards."

compensating artists. Labels employ musicians—though they technically claim not to. Labels exploit musicians by not paying or underpaying them for their work. Then Labels claim MSPs do not compensate musicians fairly. Here I want to point back to major label equity in Spotify—labels received money from Spotify from the work of their artists without distributing those funds to their own creators. Portnow made the above statement to introduce the lobbying arm of the Recording Academy, the Grammy Creators Alliance, and the effort to lobby Congress to make things "fair." However, Portnow failed to mention the organization's concern was the safe harbor policy and its impact on labels.

The Grammy Awards in 2015 was only the beginning of the lobbying against YouTube. In 2017, at a meeting of the World Intellectual Property Organization (WIPO), the IFPI's director of Insights and Analysis David Price admitted that piracy was no longer the biggest threat to the recording industry. Instead, Price stated that the biggest threat is safe harbor, which allows platforms like YouTube not to be held accountable for the content posted on their platform.[59] According to Intellectual Property Watch, his accusation stated platforms like YouTube "take advantage of the safe harbour legislations to protect themselves from negotiating fair licences with right holders."[60] For Price, YouTube hides behind safe harbor while profiting from people who post un-licensed content, even if YouTube ultimately removes access to the material. "The effect of the value gap is reflected in the dramatic mismatch between the volume of music streamed globally and the rewards that this is generating for rights holders."[61] Note here the concern is for "rights holders." While this sounds like it might be about the musicians who record music, record labels are the rights holders in this sentence. However, hidden in this rhetoric is the fact that labels pay their recording artists, not MSPs. Recall in Chapter 3, I laid out the way record contracts work. The vast majority of recording artists do not receive payment for the work they do to record an album, and this is not related to the amount retailers pay to artists, but rather how record labels distribute funds to their signees. In fact, the value gap is a complete misdiagnosis about how workers receive payment for their work under capitalism.

---

59 Saez, "YouTube And Others Hide Behind Safe Harbours, Bigger Threat Than Piracy, Music Industry Tells WIPO"; Malcolm, "Recording Industry Claims Imaginary Value Gap as a Bigger Threat Than Piracy."
60 Saez, "YouTube And Others Hide Behind Safe Harbours, Bigger Threat Than Piracy, Music Industry Tells WIPO."
61 IFPI, "Global Music Report," 8.

Not All Streams Are Equal

For all the rhetoric about how streaming is killing music, the major record labels are doing okay. The IFPI reported $29.6 billion in global revenue in 2024, $7 billion more than the previous peak in 2001.[62] According to the IFPI's own numbers, recorded music is making more money than ever. As I've argued elsewhere, their reporting is always skewed to embrace the piracy panic narrative.[63] It is a big deal for the IFPI to admit the recording industry is doing so well. However, not every MSP is equal, and the recording industry has continually changed the folk devil in their panic narrative to pressure various MSPs at different times.

Record labels claim the freemium model offered by Spotify is sufficient compensation, but those same labels fail to mention their equity deals with Spotify—equity partners can't criticize the business plan of their own investment. "They fail to recognize the agency of music corporations in the platform economy, particularly given their extensive stakes in music streaming platforms such as Spotify."[64] In the case of Spotify, the IFPI isn't concerned about compensation for their labels' artists.

Even though a stream is a stream for the end-user, *Billboard* counts different streams differently due to the revenue they produce.[65] In 2018, *Billboard* began a point system for the Hot 100 (singles chart) where subscription streams receive 1 point, ad-supported streams receive two-thirds of a point, and programmed streams receive half of a point.[66] This means that the amount of money a listener spends to hear a stream changes the non-monetary value of a stream. *Billboard* never ranked music based on revenue before. A label charging $10 for one album and $15 for another album scored the same amount on the charts based on the number of sales (not the value of the sale). At the same time, *Billboard* modified the Billboard 200 (albums chart) to count 1,200 subscription streams as one equivalent album sold and 3,750 ad-supported streams as an album, but no YouTube streams counted. In 2019, *Billboard* began counting official streams on YouTube, but not unofficial

---

62 IFPI, "IFPI"; "SoundScan 2002 Year-End Music Industry Report."
63 Arditi, "The Global Music Report: Selling a Narrative of Decline"; Arditi, "The Recording Industry in Numbers: A Record Label Centered View of Recorded Music."
64 Leyshon and Watson, "User as Asset, Music as Liability."
65 Staff, "Billboard Finalizes Changes to How Streams Are Weighted for Billboard Hot 100 & Billboard 200."
66 Wang, "Music's New Chart Rules Care – a Lot – About Whether You're Paying to Listen."

streams.[67] This means that genres and artists popular on free MSPs count less (or not all). By directly equating streams with monetary value, the recording industry reestablishes democratic consumption in the streaming era. Why does it matter? Artists at the top of the charts end up selling more music because the charts act as free advertising in themselves—this is part of the reason why *Billboard* started using SoundScan in the 1992.[68] Streams count only if they make money for labels, and the *Billboard* charts only represent revenue generating modes of consumption further linking music popularity with capitalist models.

The recording industry constructs panic narratives not to pursue criminal activity, but rather to make sure their preferred business models succeed.

---

67 Rolli, "The Billboard 200 Will Incorporate YouTube Streams In 2020"; Staff, "Billboard 200 to Include Official Video Plays From YouTube, Streaming Services."
68 Watkins, *Hip Hop Matters: Politics, Pop Culture, and the Struggle for the Soul of a Movement.*

Chapter 5

CONCLUSION: RECORD LABELS KILLED MUSIC

When Thomas Edison invented the phonograph, he didn't know people would want to listen to music on the device, much less did he know he would change the way we produce and listen to music for over a century. Our music consumption has changed ever since. At each moment of change, record labels try to convince the public of the importance of their business models by claiming music will die. Far more interesting than what happens to record labels is what happens to the music they produce based on the technologies available for production, distribution, and consumption, and why record labels make the decisions they make about how to use those technologies.

The problem with recorded music isn't the technology, but rather the decisions people make about the use of technology. Technology has affordances, which means people create technologies for specific reasons. Ultimately, people (and businesses) decide how to use technologies and the ways to develop derivative technologies. In other words, people are at the center of how and why specific technologies are created, produced, and sold to consumers. When people develop new recording technologies, they do so with an understanding that the recording industry aims to profit from the release of music. Therefore, every decision in the recording industry is driven by a capitalist profit motive.

Good music is music that sells. Or at least that is the dominant logic within the recording industry as it adheres to democratic consumption. Popular music has been a commodity since labels started selling music to be played on gramophones. With every new mediation, labels find a way to further profit from recorded music. Labels measure the popularity of any given recording not only by what people want to hear, but also by what people with expendable income want to hear. Record executives ensure every new recording technology creates profits for record labels by forcing music fans to consume music through their preferred methods.

By placing consumption as the determinant source of value, labels assume musical value emerges from money. This has had a series of effects on the music available in the market. For instance, in early Rock & Roll history, labels wanted to market rock music to a broad affluent audience, but selling music by Black artists to white consumers didn't work in the pre-civil rights era. As a result, labels fawned over artists such as Elvis to make Rock & Roll more palatable to white consumers.[1] Or later, mixtapes became the dominant way to circulate hip hop recordings. It wasn't until 1992, when *Billboard* changed the way it measures sales, that labels recognized the profit potential of hip hop music. Then labels realized the largest consumer of Black music could be white kids in the suburbs.[2]

To state the problem simply: music fans didn't kill music, record labels killed music. When Neil Portnow feigned caring about musician livelihoods at the 2015 Grammys Awards Show (discussed in Chapter 4), he failed to mention the recording industry's overall interest in selling music as a commodity rather than the music itself. In the 2006 documentary *Before the Music Dies* (*B4MD*), director Andrew Shapter shows how a set of business decisions shaped contemporary popular music.[3] Themes explored in the documentary include: female artists' sexualized appearance, producing music on a quarterly sales calendar, radio's business model, and the use of autotune. A constant refrain in the film is the idea that Bob Dylan wouldn't be popular in 2006 because label and radio executives would not have given his music the time and attention to gain popularity. The message was plain, music industry executives don't care about music, they care about profits.

To continue to profit from new media formats, the major record labels engage in panic narratives. As the shift away from piracy occurred with streaming services, the labels showed their cards by creating a new panic narrative about the value gap. With each panic narrative, major record labels, IFPI, RIAA, and BPI project their concerns about profit onto musicians. In order for people to enjoy music by their favorite artists, fans must consume music the way the recording industry says to consume it. Unfortunately, record label profits always come at the expense of pay to artists.

While record labels continue to implicate fans in the death of music, there are very real changes happening to popular music. Here, I discuss how music is compressed, shortened, and reliant on social networks of popularity. Then I turn to the latest folk devil "artificial intelligence" and the way record labels posit a panic narrative while at the same time using it to profit further from

---

1 Schaap, van der Waal, and de Koster, "Black Rap, White Rock"; Harrison, "Racial Authenticity in Rap Music and Hip Hop"; Taylor, "Funky White Boys and Honorary Soul Sisters"; Coddington, "Formatting Race on Commercial Radio Stations."
2 Watkins, *Hip Hop Matters: Politics, Pop Culture, and the Struggle for the Soul of a Movement.*
3 *B4MD*.

labor. We are in a new era of cultural creation and the boundary lines are forming, but there is much to be lost if the recording industry sets the terms of debate.

What Has Happened to Music

Over the roughly 250 years since Edison invented the phonograph, recording technologies have changed and so have the cultural practices of writing and creating music. However, the key is to remember people make decisions about how to produce and perform music in society. These decisions have a profound impact on the aesthetic and cultural experience of listening to music. In the following sections, I explore ways the recording industry has "killed" music in the digital and streaming eras.

Sounds

For all the consternation about Napster, the mp3 had a far greater impact on the sound of music than file-sharing. An mp3 is a compressed sound file that uses an algorithm to approximate the important sounds the human ear hears in uncompressed analog music. Jonathan Sterne explores the problems of mp3s in *MP3: The Meaning of a Format* (2012) as a psychoacoustic experiment that aims to eliminate sounds that our ears eliminate in the first place.[4] But the important point is that compressed sound is not the same as uncompressed sound because algorithmic compression makes decisions about what the ear hears and what is needed. It's one of the reasons for the vinyl boom,[5] where analog sound recordings produce a broad range of sound along with the comforting crackle of the record player's needle. While many vinyl collectors believe vinyl records sound better than other formats, they are correct that they have higher fidelity than most digital formats available online. However, digital technology has the potential to produce fuller sounding music than any vinyl record; this is the reason classical music fans were so eager to adopt the CD.

Furthermore, as producers have become more dependent on digital audio workstations (DAWs), they have deployed technology in a way to change the sounds of music.[6] Whereas analog recordings allowed splicing tape to edit

---

4 Sterne, *MP3*.
5 Palm, "Analog Backlog"; Palm, "The New Old: Vinyl Records after the Internet"; Skrimsjö, "Standing in the Way of Control"; Leight, "Vinyl Is Poised to Outsell CDs For the First Time Since 1986."
6 Frith and Zagorski-Thomas, *The Art of Record Production*.

together different recordings, not much could be done about wrong notes or off rhythm. DAWs not only permitted producers to splice recordings easily, but also made it easier to change notes and quantize rhythm to align it with the beat. These are useful tools, but the major record labels' desire to cut budgets has led to smaller studio staffs who use digital tools to cut corners and increase profits.

Choices

Capitalism prides itself on choice, but choice is only available when capitalists believe there is a market for it. I am reminded of this every time I go to the grocery store and certain products, I regularly buy, are no longer available, while they are available at other stores. Grocery store managers make decisions about my choices based on what sells in the store, but consumers can only purchase what is available on the shelves. The same is true in the recording industry. We don't have infinite choices in music because music gatekeepers (musicians, producers, A&R staff, executives, MSPs) make decisions about what people want to hear.

For example, Pandora's music genome project made it feel as though platforms gave us the capacity to find the music we like. Despite years of feeling like we have access to unlimited music, our choices are becoming quite limited. First, the surveillance of music creates a situation where our choices become exploited by record labels.[7] Then, those patterns themselves become more similar. Whereas genres feel different, their differences are only to the extent to which they can be exploited for marketing.[8] More concerningly, as algorithms choose what we want to hear, and we feel they do a good job, we close ourselves to other music we don't know we would like. Record labels actively use algorithms to analyze user data to make decisions about what to record.[9] On one level this is the same process of pseudo-individuation[10] Theodor Adorno and Max Horkheimer discussed. The choices presented to us are the result of our desires, but those choices are decided by culture industry executives who need shortcuts. On another level, this system creates the desires of those who listen. When the algorithms effectively pick music for us, they make us happy, but we also don't know what we're missing, which separates us from our true happiness.

---

7 Drott, "Surveillance of and through Music."
8 Coddington, "Formatting Race on Commercial Radio Stations"; Negus, *Music Genres and Corporate Cultures*; Poole, "Sorted."
9 Tolstad, "'The Numbers Don't Lie!'"
10 Horkheimer and Adorno, "The Culture Industry: Enlightenment as Mass Deception."

Shorter songs

Recording technology shapes culture. Much like the implementation of mp3s produced flatter-sounding music, recording technology and MSPs have shortened the length of music. In 1934, Theodor Adorno wrote "the only thing that can characterize gramophone music is the inevitable brevity dictated by the size of the shellac plate."[11] Adorno's perspective followed the widespread adoption of 78 rpm records. These records only permitted approximately 2.5–3 min of music per side of the record. Before the phonograph/gramophone, music wasn't limited by time. I always picture the absurdity of trying to record Beethoven's Symphony No. 9. The 70-min symphony would take roughly 28 record sides at 2.5 min per side. Someone would have to consistently switch recording gramophones as the orchestra played. The result would be roughly 14 records all cutting off in the middle of musical phrases. On the other end of the spectrum, a popular song could be performed for as long as the performer desired. In either case, the music could not be adapted easily to the recording format. For nearly a century, after long play (LP) vinyl, cassettes, CDs, and mp3s allowed music to be considerably longer, the average length of a song remained about 3 min in length.

However, the length of songs is changing once again, and they are getting shorter. Songs are becoming shorter with quicker hooks because of the commodity form of music. Technology has affordances—a possibility enabled by a particular technical artifact—but people quickly adopt cultural positions connected to what they are used to hearing. From the shortness of 78 rpm records to the algorithms of Spotify, music is limited by technology, yes, but every technology is made with intentions by people. According to an analysis by Szu Yu Chen for *The Washington Post*, pop songs averaged 2:46 in the 1950s, peaked at 4:14 in the 1990s, and now average 3:15 in the 2020s.[12] In the same analysis, she found that one-fifth of 2024's Grammy-nominated songs lasted less than 3 minutes buoyed by NewJeans' single "NewJeans" at 1 minute and 48 seconds.[13] Additionally, Lil' Yachty's 2022 hit "Poland" clocked in at 1:23. Even the idea that one-fifth of Grammy-nominated songs came in under 3 minutes is an undercount because some Grammy-nominated songs are in areas like jazz, classical, and film music, which are unlikely to be affected by the changes in music streaming.

Producers and record label staff guide recording artists on the lengths of their songs based on the market and technology available at the time. Spotify,

---

11 Adorno, "The Form of the Phonograph Record," 278.
12 Szu Yu Chen, "Pop Songs Are Getting Shorter in the Era of Streaming and TikTok."
13 Ibid.

Apple Music, and YouTube all count a stream after the listener streams for 30 seconds. So the goal of the recording industry is to get streamers to listen for at least 30 seconds, but there are diminishing returns if someone listens to a long song. If a song is 5 minutes, then that represents at least eight additional streams of lost opportunity cost because streamers could have listened to more songs and generated more streams. Someone listening to Lil' Yachty's "Poland" can go listen to another Lil' Yachty song earning more streams. The result isn't just a technically shorter song, but also a structurally different posture toward recording music. Artists are releasing music with fewer intros with an emphasis on catchy hooks early on to catch listeners' attention to pass the 30-second mark. A slow intro may lose listeners as they skip the track. Record labels are killing music by making songs shorter.

Social Media Virality

Pop music has never been about the sound of music, per se. Instead, people tend to listen to music that gets their attention whether from the appearance of the performers to something they identify with politically or socially. Take for example Psy's "Gangnam Style," which became a viral hit in late 2012. The song was everywhere, and people kept saying "Gangnam Style" and doing the invisible horse dance. However, I never spoke to anyone who thought the song was a banger. "Gangnam Style" was the first meme song.

Following Psy's success, a long list of artists have risen to fame through social media virality.[14] Lil Nas X became the champion of meme culture and an overnight pop star sensation with the release of his song "Old Town Road" in 2018. Having never recorded or performed a song live before, Lil Nas X's "Old Town Road" became the longest running number one song on the *Billboard* Hot 100 in chart history.[15] Then influencers like Bella Poarch, Megan Maroney, Benson Boone, and Addison Rae used social media to rocket to fame. These influencers used TikTok, Instagram, Twitter, and YouTube to create a following, then they translated followers into record contracts. At no point is there concern about the sound of these influencers' music for the labels that sign them, but rather the only concern labels have is the number of conversions from social media interactions to MSP streams.

TikTok is the major social media folk devil of the recording industry today. Whereas other social media websites do not easily facilitate music

---

14 Sampson, *Virality*.
15 Eells, "Lil Nas X"; Avdeeff, "Lil Nas X, TikTok, and the Evolution of Music Engagement on Social Networking Sites."

distribution (except YouTube, depending on how you characterize it), TikTok began with music at its core. Beginning with Music.ly, TikTok's predecessor, music was the site's mission as the site began as a lip-syncing tool. At that time, record labels expressed issues about the app for copyright issues, but Music.ly purposefully made the videos so short that they did not violate copyright law. Early on, record labels began paying influencers to lip sync to their music as a way of marketing new music. After ByteDance purchased the site in 2017 and merged it with TikTok in 2018, the importance of getting a song on the platform to go viral only increased. Now marketing music on TikTok is a crucial element for labels and artists, but the marketing doesn't translate directly into a hit song,[16] partly because the videos are too short to count as streams.

Furthermore, social media becomes work. As Andrew Leyshon and Alan Watson state "it seems clear that developing and maintaining an online presence involves an entrepreneurial approach to self-marketing and brings new (and often invisible and unpaid) demands in the shape of relational labour."[17] Social media becomes work because artists now need to promote themselves online to garner attention (and views and streams).[18] While this creates skills applicable to other fields of employment,[19] it creates hours of additional unpaid labor that ultimately benefits the recording industry and silicon valley.

Algorithmic Exploitation

> "SWEEPING across the country with the speed of a transient fashion in slang or Panama hats, political war cries or popular novels, comes now the mechanical device to sing for us a song or play for us a piano, in substitute for human skill, intelligence, and soul."[20] – John Philip Sousa

In John Philip Sousa's words, a scary technological threat is sweeping the United States hell-bent on destroying music. Sousa's folk devil is the gramophone, but you can hear the echoes of different technological transformations that took place over the next 120 years. From gramophones

---

16 Leight, "The Challenge of Marketing Music on TikTok in 2024."
17 Leyshon and Watson, *The Rise of the Platform Music Industries*.
18 Arditi, *Getting Signed*; Watson, Watson, and Tompkins, "Does Social Media Pay for Music Artists?"
19 Watkins, *Don't Knock the Hustle*; Lee, *Blowin' Up*.
20 Sousa, "The Menace of Mechanical Music."

to DAWs to artificial intelligence (AI) each new technology is viewed as the loss of something creative. People still play brass instruments and perform Sousa's famous marches. While many producers use DAWs, others insist on analog recording technology (see Leon Bridge's *Coming Home*). And despite the fear of AI, music will still be produced and performed by humans. In Chapter 4, I discussed the panic that there may be no new artists due to the "value gap," but of course, there will be new music because people always want to play and listen to music. However, each change does have a real impact as businesses seek ways to eliminate labor. I think we need to be cautious about, if not resistant to, the deployment of AI, but I think major labels will deploy AI to undercut the value of labor while the industry fights other people deploying the technology.

Labor is experiencing an upheaval for high-skill creative and white-collar workers because of AI. However, AI is a marketing term that obfuscates the actual technology. Since the goal of these technologies is to replace high-skilled labor with low-skilled labor, I prefer the term algorithmic exploitation (AE). Exploitation is the amount of unpaid value workers create without compensation. This is the reason businesses are quickly adopting AI before the technology is ready for use: to reduce the level of skill needed to do a job. AE emphasizes the fact that these programs run algorithms. People make algorithms for specific purposes and in the case of AE music, it will be deployed by labels to cut labor.

In an interesting way, AE music eliminates the means of production for commercial music because music created with algorithms can be produced for the price of a computer and internet access. Copyright was the original way labels separated musicians from the means of production. Musicians trade the rights to their music for an advance in their record contract. File-sharing and social media made inroads to disintermediate this process, but streaming acted to reintermediate[21] the process through MSPs. To keep copyright as the central means of production, record labels feel they need to fight AI while using AE. Maintaining gatekeepers allows major record labels to sustain the recording industry's dominance in the broader music industry.

Therefore, it is not surprising for copyright to be the tool the recording industry uses to wage its battle against AI. Recently, a US federal appeals court ruled that AI music can't be copyrighted because it does not have an author.[22] However, uncopyrightable music can't make labels money, this is

---

21 Watson and Leyshon, "Negotiating Platformisation"; Leyshon and Watson, *The Rise of the Platform Music Industries*.
22 Brittain, "US Appeals Court Rejects Copyrights for AI-Generated Art Lacking 'human' Creator."

their underlying opposition to AI music. At the same time, they claim AI steals copyright. The Recording Industry Association of America (RIAA), along with Sony Music Entertainment, Warner Records, and Universal Music Group, sued Suno and Udio, two generative AI services, because they argue these services learned from copyrighted material.[23] Labels and the RIAA argue that feeding Suno and Udio copyrighted material without a license is an unauthorized reproduction. Under their logic, we all violate copyright every time we listen to music because musicians learn to play instruments by playing other music—rarely do they pay for the score.

However, companies will find a way to profit from the creation of AI music by deploying it as AE music—i.e., AI designed to undercut musicians in the production process. For instance, hit music producer, Timbaland, began using Suno to produce his music.[24] Timbaland can create thousands of tracks on his laptop without using any other studio labor. After complaining about the use of his voice on an AE track, Drake used AE to replicate Tupac and Snoop Dogg's voices in a diss-track.[25] These are the obvious instances as countless songwriters use ChatGPT to come up with lyrics and themes for their music. As more artists and labels use AE to eliminate labor, it will become increasingly difficult to cut AE from the process. Instead, labels, producers, and artists will use AE to eliminate labor from music making.

But a key point is that just because people use AI to make music, doesn't mean we will want to listen to it. Despite the current panic narratives about AI, people will always make music, and the human element will always be important in its creation. In other words, just because a computer can produce music doesn't mean anyone wants to hear it—or if they do want to hear it, that there is anything wrong with them or the music. However, it is always important to remember that labels will use AE to reduce labor in the production process.

Record labels will continue to produce new panic narratives to alter music policy and public opinion for each new technology for the music production, distribution, and consumption of music. By arguing fans and technology are killing music, the recording industry ignores the role record labels play in destroying musical creativity. In an ironic way, the industry's music panic narratives that discuss the death of music ignore the live/dead

---

23 Aswad, "Major Labels Sue AI Music Services Suno and Udio for Copyright Infringement."
24 Hiatt, "Timbaland's AI Reinvention."
25 Levine, "Did Drake Use AI to Say FU to Artists' Rights?"

binary. Recorded music was always dead when compared to "live" music. Seen from this perspective, recorded music is always-already dead music. Their use of death aims to scare music fans while ignoring the long history of musical culture that exists without recordings. It is vital to push back against the recording industry's rhetoric to find a way to separate music from label interests. Panic narratives are tools used to create profit, not to protect music.

BIBLIOGRAPHY

"57th Annual *Grammy Awards*." Grammy Awards. Los Angeles: CBS, February 8, 2015.
ABC News. "The Home Video Prince Doesn't Want You to See," February 18, 2009. https://abcnews.go.com/TheLaw/home-video-prince/story?id=3777651.
Adorno, Theodor W. "The Form of the Phonograph Record." In *Essays on Music/ Theodor W. Adorno*, edited by Theodor W. Adorno, Richard D. Leppert, and Susan H. Gillespie, 277–280. Berkeley, CA: University of California Press, 2002.
Aglietta, Michel. *A Theory of Capitalist Regulation: The US Experience*, translated by David Fernbach. New edition. New York, NY: Verso, 2001.
Ahmed, Sahnun. "Somali Piracy 2.0 – The Angry Fishermen on the High Seas." *BBC*, December 22, 2024. https://www.bbc.com/news/articles/cq8vl8n9gypo.
Ahrens, Frank. "Stars Come Out Against Net Music Piracy in New Ads." *Washington Post*. September 26, 2002, Final edition, sec. A.
Al-Rafee, Sulaiman, and Timothy Paul Cronan. "Digital Piracy: Factors That Influence Attitude toward Behavior." *Journal of Business Ethics* 63, no. 3 (2006): 237–259. doi:10.2307/25123707.
Ambrosino, Brandon. "Aerosmith Made More Money from 'Guitar Hero' than from Any One of Its Albums." *Vox*, July 11, 2014. https://www.vox.com/2014/7/11/5890237/aerosmith-made-more-money-from-guitar-hero-than-from-any-one-of-its-albums.
Anderson, Tim J. *Popular Music in a Digital Music Economy: Problems and Practices for an Emerging Service Industry*. New York: Routledge, 2014.
Anderton, Chris, and James Hannam. "Pressing Reset: Reimagining Performer and Songwriter Revenues in the Contemporary Music Industry." In *The Palgrave Handbook of Critical Music Industry Studies*, edited by David Arditi and Ryan Nolan, 49–68. Cham: Springer Nature Switzerland, 2024. doi:10.1007/978-3-031-64013-1_4.
Anderton, Chris, and Sergio Pisfil, eds. *Researching Live Music: Gigs, Tours, Concerts and Festivals*. 1st edition. New York, N.Y.: Focal Press, 2021.
Arditi, David. Criminalizing Independent Music: The Recording Industry Association of America's Advancement of Dominant Ideology. VDM Verlag, 2007.
———. "Digital Downsizing: The Effects of Digital Music Production on Labor." *Journal of Popular Music Studies* 26, no. 4 (2014): 503–520.
———. "Digital Subscriptions: The Unending Consumption of Music in the Digital Era." *Popular Music and Society* 41, no. 3 (2018): 302–18. doi:10.1080/03007766.2016.1264101.
———. "Disciplining the Consumer: File-Sharers under the Watchful Eye of the Music Industry." In *Internet and Surveillance: The Challenges of Web 2.0 and Social Media*, edited by Christian Fuchs, Kees Boersma, Anders Albrechtslund, and Marisol Sandoval, pp. 170–186. New York, NY: Routledge, 2011.

———. "Downloading Is Killing Music: The Recording Industry's Piracy Panic Narrative." In *Civilisations*, edited by Victor Sarafian and Rosemary Findley, pp. 13–32. The State of the Music Industry, vol. 63, no. 1, 2014.

———. *Getting Signed: Record Contracts, Musicians, and Power in Society*. New York, NY: Palgrave Macmillan, 2020. doi:10.1007/978-3-030-44587-4.

———. "Introduction: Napster at 25." *Fast Capitalism* 21, no. 1 (October 29, 2024). https://fastcapitalism.journal.library.uta.edu/index.php/fastcapitalism/article/view/512.

———. *iTake-Over: The Recording Industry in the Digital Era*. Lanham, MD: Rowman & Littlefield Publishers, 2014.

———. *iTake-Over: The Recording Industry in the Streaming Era*. 2nd edition. Lanham, MD: Lexington Books, 2020.

———. "iTunes: Breaking Barriers and Building Walls." *Popular Music and Society* 37, no. 4 (2014): 408–424.

———. "Music Everywhere: Setting a Digital Music Trap." *Critical Sociology* 45, nos. 4–5 (2019): 617–630. doi:10.1177/0896920517729192.

———. "Musicians, Labor, and COVID19." *Blog. Working in Music*, June 9, 2020. https://wim.hypotheses.org/1352.

———. "On Competition in Music." In *Getting Signed: Record Contracts, Musicians, and Power in Society*, edited by David Arditi, pp. 119–148. Cham: Springer International Publishing, 2020. doi:10.1007/978-3-030-44587-4_5.

———. "Policing Piracy: The Piracy Panic Narrative from Napster to Spotify." In *Annual Meeting of the Cultural Studies Association*. Philadelphia, PA, 2016.

———. "Record Contracts: Recording Artists, Work, and Exploitation." In *The Palgrave Handbook of Critical Music Industry Studies*, edited by David Arditi and Ryan Nolan, pp. 83–95. New York, NY: Palgrave Macmillan, 2024. doi:10.1007/978-3-031-64013-1_6.

———. *Streaming Culture: Subscription Platforms and the Unending Consumption of Culture*. SocietyNow. New Milford, CT: Emerald Publishing Limited, 2021.

———. "Synergy and Syncs: Record Labels, Video Games, and Unending Consumption." In *The Oxford Handbook of Video Game Music and Sound*, edited by William Gibbons and Mark Grimshaw-Aagaard, pp. 399–412. New York, NY: Oxford University Press, 2024. doi:10.1093/oxfordhb/9780197556160.013.43.

———. "The Global Music Report: Selling a Narrative of Decline." In *Music by Numbers: The Use and Abuse of Statistics in the Music Industry*, edited by Richard Osborne and Dave Laing, 74–89. Chicago, IL: Intellect Ltd, 2021.

———. *The Recording Industry in Numbers: A Record Label Centered View of Recorded Music*, February 14, 2015. https://itakeoverbook.wordpress.com/2015/02/14/the-recording-industry-in-numbers-a-record-label-centered-view-of-recorded-music/.

———. "The State of Music: Cultural, Political and Economic Transformations in the Music Industry." Dissertation, George Mason University, 2012.

———. "Video Game Concerts: Unending Consumption on Video Game Platforms." *Critical Sociology*, February 4, 2024, 08969205241229064. doi:10.1177/08969205241229064.

Ashworth, Boone. "The Whole of the 'Whole Earth Catalog' Is Now Online." *Wired*, October 13, 2023. https://www.wired.com/story/whole-earth-catalog-now-online-internet-archive/.

Association of Research Libraries. "Copyright Timeline: A History of Copyright in the United States." *Association of Research Libraries*. March 28, 2025. https://www.arl.org/copyright-timeline/.
Aswad, Jem. "Major Labels Sue AI Music Services Suno and Udio for Copyright Infringement." *Variety*, June 24, 2024. https://variety.com/2024/music/news/record-labels-sue-ai-music-services-suno-and-udio-copyright-infringement-1236045366/.
———. "Vinyl Sales Soar — and Even CDs Rebound — as U.S. Recorded Music Industry Posts $15 Billion Year-End Revenue." *Variety*, March 9, 2022. https://variety.com/2022/music/news/vinyl-sales-riaa-revenue-2021-year-end-1235199997/.
Attali, Jacques. Noise: The Political Economy of Music. *Theory and History of Literature*. Minneapolis: University of Minnesota Press, 1985.
Avdeeff, Melissa. "Lil Nas X, TikTok, and the Evolution of Music Engagement on Social Networking Sites." In *Virtual Identities and Digital Culture*, edited by Victoria Kannen and Aaron Langille. Abingdon, UK: Routledge, 2023.
Baker, C. Edwin. *Media Concentration and Democracy: Why Ownership Matters. Communication, Society, and Politics*. New York: Cambridge University Press, 2007.
———. *Media, Markets, and Democracy. Communication, Society, and Politics*. Cambridge; New York: Cambridge University Press, 2002. http://www.loc.gov/catdir/description/cam021/2001025498.html, http://www.loc.gov/catdir/toc/cam026/2001025498.html.
Bangeman, Eric. "'I Sue Dead People....'" *Ars Technica*, February 4, 2005. https://arstechnica.com/uncategorized/2005/02/4587-2/.
Barbrook, Richard, and Andy Cameron. "The Californian Ideology." *Science as Culture* 6 (1996): 44–72.
Bareilles, Sara. Love Song. Little Voice. *Epic*, 2007. https://genius.com/Sara-bareilles-love-song-lyrics.
Becker, Howard Saul. *Art Worlds*. 1st ed. Berkeley, CA: University of California Press, 1984.
Before the Music Dies. DVD, Documentary. Roadwings Entertainment, 2006.
Behrendtz, Jörgen. "Convenience Begets Capitalism." *Fast Capitalism* 21, no. 1 (2024). https://fastcapitalism.journal.library.uta.edu/index.php/fastcapitalism/article/view/500.
Benkler, Yochai. *The Wealth of Networks: How Social Production Transforms Markets and Freedom*. New Haven, CT: Yale University Press, 2006.
Bennett, Toby. *Corporate Life in the Digital Music Industry: Remaking the Major Record Label from the Inside Out*. New York: Bloomsbury Academic, 2024.
Billboard. "Billboard 200 Makeover: Album Chart to Incorporate Streams & Track Sales," November 19, 2014. http://www.billboard.com/articles/columns/chart-beat/6320099/billboard-200-makeover-streams-digital-tracks.
Blau, Justine. "Music Biz Sues Student File-Swappers." *CBS News*, April 4, 2003. https://www.cbsnews.com/news/music-biz-sues-student-file-swappers-04-04-2003/.
Breen, Marcus. "Napster 'Freedom' at Northeastern University: A Distanced Ethnography." *Fast Capitalism* 21, no. 1 (2024). https://fastcapitalism.journal.library.uta.edu/index.php/fastcapitalism/article/view/503.
Brittain, Blake. "US Appeals Court Rejects Copyrights for AI-Generated Art Lacking 'human' Creator." *Reuters*, March 18, 2025, sec. United States. https://www.reuters.com/world/us/us-appeals-court-rejects-copyrights-ai-generated-art-lacking-human-creator-2025-03-18/.

Broder, David S., and Thomas B. Edsall. "Clinton Finds Biracial Support for Criticism of Rap Singer." *The Washington Post*, June 16, 1992. https://www.washingtonpost.com/archive/politics/1992/06/16/clinton-finds-biracial-support-for-criticism-of-rap-singer/5cca24ae-0e01-4641-afe6-f10a3fc8a42a/.

Bruno, Antony. "Beatles Catalog Finally Coming to iTunes, Apple Announces." *Billboard*, November 16, 2010. /bbcomnews/beatles-catalog-finally-coming-to-itunes-1004126881.story.

Burgess, Jean, and Joshua Green. *YouTube: Online Video and Participatory Culture. 1 edition*. Cambridge, Malden, MA: Polity, 2009.

Burkart, Patrick. "Music in the Cloud and the Digital Sublime." *Popular Music and Society* 37, no. 4 (2013): 393–407. doi:10.1080/03007766.2013.810853.

———. *Pirate Politics: The New Information Policy Contests*. Cambridge, MA: The MIT Press, 2014. doi:10.7551/mitpress/9205.001.0001.

Burkart, Patrick, and Tom McCourt. *Digital Music Wars: Ownership and Control of the Celestial Jukebox*. New York: Rowman & Littlefield Publishers, 2006.

Burns, Jehnie I. *Mixtape Nostalgia: Culture, Memory, and Representation*. Lanham: Lexington Books, 2021.

Coddington, Amy. "Formatting Race on Commercial Radio Stations." In *The Palgrave Handbook of Critical Music Industry Studies*, edited by David Arditi and Ryan Nolan, pp. 255–71. Cham: Springer Nature Switzerland, 2024. doi:10.1007/978-3-031-64013-1_16.

Cohen, Stanley. *Folk Devils and Moral Panics: The Creation of the Mods and Rockers*. New York: Routledge, 2011. http://public.eblib.com/EBLPublic/PublicView.do?ptiID=684015.

Copyright Alliance. "DMCA Safe Harbor | Copyright Alliance." *Copyright Alliance: Create, Innovate, Protect*. May 13, 2025. https://copyrightalliance.org/education/copyright-law-explained/the-digital-millennium-copyright-act-dmca/dmca-safe-harbor/.

Cording, Jess. "Study Shows 16 Million People Learned To Play Guitar During The First Two Years Of The Pandemic." *Forbes*, June 24, 2022. https://www.forbes.com/sites/jesscording/2022/06/24/study-shows-16-million-people-learned-to-play-guitar-during-the-first-two-years-of-the-pandemic/.

Cornelius-Bell, Aidan. "A Capitalist Stranglehold on 'Artificial Intelligence': A Gallop through Piracy, Privacy Invasion, Lock-in and a Fever Dream of Democratisation." *Fast Capitalism* 21, no. 1 (2024). https://fastcapitalism.journal.library.uta.edu/index.php/fastcapitalism/article/view/499.

Cornish, Audie, Stephanie Lenz, and Daniel Nazer. "Appeals Court Rules Youtube Video Of Baby Dancing To Prince Was Fair Use." *NPR*, September 15, 2015. https://www.npr.org/2015/09/15/440621419/appeals-court-rules-youtube-video-of-baby-dancing-to-prince-was-fair-use.

David, Matthew. *Peer to Peer and the Music Industry: The Criminalization of Sharing*. Los Angeles: Sage Publications Ltd, 2010.

Dibbell, Julian. "The New Face of Music Piracy." *Rolling Stone*, June 8, 2000.

FBI. "Download the FBI's Anti-Piracy Warning Seal." August 8, 2013. http://www.fbi.gov/about-us/investigate/white_collar/ipr/download-the-fbis-anti-piracy-warning-seal.

Dozal, Mario. "Consumerism Hero: The 'Selling Out' of Guitar Hero and Rock Band." In *Music Video Games: Performance, Politics, and Play*, edited by Michael Austin, pp. 127–152. New York: Bloomsbury Academic, 2016.

Drew, Rob. "New Technologies and the Business of Music: Lessons from the 1980s Home Taping Hearings." *Popular Music and Society*, February 8, 2013, 1–20.

———. *Unspooled: How the Cassette Made Music Shareable*. Durham: Duke University Press Books, 2024.

Drott, Eric. "Surveillance of and through Music." In *The Palgrave Handbook of Critical Music Industry Studies*, edited by David Arditi and Ryan Nolan, pp. 273–289. Cham: Springer Nature Switzerland, 2024. doi:10.1007/978-3-031-64013-1_17.

Edge, Ruth, Leonard Petts, and Ruth Guide to collecting His master's voice "Nipper" souvenirs Edge. *The Collectors Guide to "His Master's Voice" Nipper Souvenirs*. London : EMI, 1997. http://archive.org/details/collectorsguidet0000ruth.

Eells, Josh. "Lil Nas X: Inside the Rise of a Hip-Hop Cowboy." *Rolling Stone*, May 20, 2019. https://www.rollingstone.com/music/music-features/lil-nas-x-old-town-road-interview-new-album-836393/.

Eriksson, Maria, Rasmus Fleischer, Anna Johansson, Pelle Snickars, and Patrick Vonderau. *Spotify Teardown: Inside the Black Box of Streaming Music*. Cambridge, MA: MIT Press, 2019.

Frith, Simon. "The Industrialization of Popular Music." In *Popular Music and Communication*, edited by James Lull, 2nd ed., 53–79. Newbury Park, CA: Sage Publications, 1992.

Frith, Simon, and Simon Zagorski-Thomas, eds. *The Art of Record Production: An Introductory Reader for a New Academic Field*. Surrey, England: Ashgate Publishing, Ltd., 2012.

Fuchs, Christian. "Dallas Smythe Today – The Audience Commodity, the Digital Labour Debate, Marxist Political Economy and Critical Theory. Prolegomena to a Digital Labour Theory of Value." *tripleC: Communication, Capitalism & Critique. Open Access Journal for a Global Sustainable Information Society* 10, no. 2 (2012): 692–740.

Galuszka, Patryk. "Showcase Festivals as a Gateway to Foreign Markets." In *Researching Live Music: Gigs, Tours, Concerts and Festivals*, edited by Chris Anderton and Sergio Pisfil, 1st edition, pp. 56–67. New York, NY: Focal Press, 2021.

Garofalo, Reebee. "I Want My MP3: Who Owns Internet Music?" In *Policing Pop*, edited by Reebee Garofalo and Martin Cloonan, pp. 30–45. Sound Matters. Philadelphia: Temple University Press, 2003.

Gay, Paul du, Stuart Hall, Linda Janes, Hugh McKay, and Keith Negus. *Doing Cultural Studies: The Story of the Sony Walkman*. 2nd ed. Los Angeles: SAGE, 2013.

Gillespie, Tarleton. *Wired Shut: Copyright and the Shape of Digital Culture*. Cambridge, MA: MIT Press, 2007.

Goode, Erich, and Nachman Ben-Yehuda. *Moral Panics: The Social Construction of Deviance*. 2nd ed. Chichester, UK: Wiley-Blackwell, 2009.

Gramsci, Antonio. "Hegemony, Relations of Force, Historical Bloc." In *Antonio Gramsci Reader*, 189–221. New York: Schocken Books, 1988.

Grazian, David. Mix It Up: Popular Culture, *Mass Media, and Society*. 2nd ed. New York, NY: W. W. Norton, Incorporated, 2017.

Hall, Stuart, and Tony Jefferson. *Resistance Through Rituals: Youth Subcultures in Post-War Britain*. London: Hutchinson, 1976.

Hampp, Andrew. "SoundCloud Debuts Monetization Play With 'On SoundCloud', Announces $100 Million In Funding." *Billboard*, August 21, 2014. https://www.billboard.com/pro/soundcloud-monetization-advertising/.

Harrell, Phil. "2 Live Crew Fought the Law with Its Album, 'As Nasty As They Wanna Be.'" *NPR*, August 10, 2023, sec. Music. https://www.npr.org/2023/08/10/1193106943/hip-hops-game-changer-2-live-crews-as-nasty-as-they-wanna-be.

Harrison, Anthony Kwame. "'Cheaper than a CD, plus We Really Mean It': Bay Area Underground Hip Hop Tapes as Subcultural Artifacts." *Popular Music* 25, no. 2 (2006): 283–301.

———. *Hip Hop Underground: The Integrity and Ethics of Racial Identification*. Philadelphia: Temple University Press, 2009.

———. "Racial Authenticity in Rap Music and Hip Hop." *Sociology Compass* 2, no. 6 (2008): 1783–1800. doi:10.1111/j.1751-9020.2008.00171.x.

Hesmondhalgh, David. "Is Music Streaming Bad for Musicians? Problems of Evidence and Argument." *New Media & Society* 23, no. 12 (2021): 3593–3615. doi:10.1177/1461444820953541.

Hesmondhalgh, David, Ellis Jones, and Andreas Rauh. "SoundCloud and Bandcamp as Alternative Music Platforms." *Social Media + Society* 5, no. 4 (2019): 2056305119883429. doi:10.1177/2056305119883429.

Hiatt, Brian. "Timbaland's AI Reinvention: 'God Presented This Tool to Me.'" *Rolling Stone*, March 19, 2025. https://www.rollingstone.com/music/music-features/timbaland-ai-artificial-intelligence-suno-music-1235297689/.

Hissong, Samantha. "Did Everyone Buy a Guitar in Quarantine or What?" *Rolling Stone*, January 28, 2021. https://www.rollingstone.com/pro/news/music-instruments-sweetwater-reverb-guitar-center-1119868/.

Holmes, David. "Artists Claim YouTube Pays Them Less Than Spotify. Are They Right?" *Fast Company*, May 9, 2016. https://www.fastcompany.com/3059507/artists-claim-youtube-pays-artists-less-than-spotify-are-they-right.

Horkheimer, Max, and Theodor W. Adorno. *Dialectic of Enlightenment*. New York: Herder and Herder, 1972.

———. "The Culture Industry: Enlightenment as Mass Deception." In *Dialectic of Enlightenment*, xvii, 258 p. New York: Herder and Herder, 1972.

Hracs, Brian J., Doreen Jakob, and Atle Hauge. "Standing Out in the Crowd: The Rise of Exclusivity-Based Strategies to Compete in the Contemporary Marketplace for Music and Fashion." *Environment and Planning A: Economy and Space* 45, no. 5 (n.d.): 1141–1161.

Hull, Geoffrey P., Thomas W. Hutchison, and Richard Strasser. *The Music Business and Recording Industry: Delivering Music in the 21st Century*. 3rd ed. New York, NY: Routledge, 2011.

Huston, Caitlin. "Spotify Adds Record Number of Users in Quarter, Paid Subscribers Hit 268M." *The Hollywood Reporter*, April 29, 2025. https://www.hollywoodreporter.com/business/digital/spotify-record-users-quarter-paid-subscribers-1236202997/.

IFPI. *Digital Music Report 2015*. International Federation of Phonographic Industries, 2015.

———. *Global Music Report 2016*. International Federation of Phonographic Industries, 2016. http://www.ifpi.org/news/IFPI-GLOBAL-MUSIC-REPORT-2016.

———. "IFPI: AMIDST HIGHLY COMPETITIVE MARKET, GLOBAL RECORDED MUSIC REVENUES GREW 4.8% IN 2024." *IFPI*, March 19, 2025. https://www.ifpi.org/ifpi-amidst-highly-competitive-market-global-recorded-music-revenues-grew-4-8-in-2024/.

———. "Recording Industry in Numbers." *International Federation of the Phonographic Industry*, 2000.

———. "Recording Industry in Numbers." *International Federation of the Phonographic Industry*, 2001.

———. "Recording Industry in Numbers." *International Federation of the Phonographic Industry*, 2002.

———. "Recording Industry in Numbers." *International Federation of the Phonographic Industry*, 2003.

———. "Recording Industry in Numbers." *International Federation of the Phonographic Industry*, 2004.

———. "Recording Industry in Numbers." *International Federation of the Phonographic Industry*, 2005.

———. "Recording Industry in Numbers." *International Federation of the Phonographic Industry*, 2008.

———. "Recording Industry in Numbers." *International Federation of the Phonographic Industry*, 2010.

———. "Recording Industry in Numbers." *International Federation of the Phonographic Industry*, 2011.

Ingham, Tim. "Here's Exactly How Many Shares the Major Labels and Merlin Bought in Spotify – and What Those Stakes Are Worth Now." *Music Business Worldwide*, May 14, 2018. https://www.musicbusinessworldwide.com/heres-exactly-how-many-shares-the-major-labels-and-merlin-bought-in-spotify-and-what-we-think-those-stakes-are-worth-now/.

———. "If Universal Music Sells Its Spotify Stock Right Now, Artists Get $500 Million." *Rolling Stone*, February 11, 2021. https://www.rollingstone.com/pro/features/universal-music-spotify-ownership-artists-1126893/.

———. "Universal Music Group's Stock in Spotify Is Worth $3bn. Time to Sell?" *Music Business Worldwide*, November 18, 2024. https://www.musicbusinessworldwide.com/universal-music-groups-stake-in-spotify-is-now-worth-3-billion-is-it-time-to-sell/.

Jhally, Sut. *The Codes of Advertising: Fetishism and the Political Economy of Meaning in the Consumer Society*. New York, NY: St. Martin's Press, 1987.

Kane, Margaret. "Dr. Dre Sues Napster -- and Users?" *ZDNET*, April 25, 2000. https://www.zdnet.com/article/dr-dre-sues-napster-and-users/.

Karp, Hannah. "Streaming Sidesteps The Labels." *Billboard*, June 16, 2018. https://go-gale-com.ezproxy.uta.edu/ps/i.do?p=ITOF&u=txshracd2597&id=GALE%7CA543899365&v=2.1&it=r&sid=summon&aty=ip.

Kelley, Robin D. G. "Without a Song: New York Musicians Strike Out against Technology." In *Three Strikes: Miners, Musicians, Salesgirls, and the Fighting Spirit of Labor's Last Century*, edited by Howard Zinn, Robin D. G. Kelley, and Dana Frank, pp. 119–156. Boston: Beacon Press, 2002.

Klein, Bethany, Giles Moss, and Lee Edwards. *Understanding Copyright: Intellectual Property in the Digital Age*. Los Angeles, California: SAGE Publications Ltd, 2015.

Knowles. "The Artificiality of Digital Scarcity: Contradictions between Code, Law, Norms, and Value(s)." *Fast Capitalism* 21, no. 1 (2024). https://fastcapitalism.journal.library.uta.edu/index.php/fastcapitalism/article/view/505.

Kraft, James P. "Musicians in Hollywood: Work and Technological Change in Entertainment Industries, 1926–1940." In *The Popular Music Studies Reader*, edited by Andy Bennett, Barry Shank, and Jason Toynbee, xxii, 408 p. London; New York: Routledge, 2006.

Krasilovsky, M. William, Sidney Shemel, John M. Gross, and Jonathan Feinstein. *This Business of Music*. 10th ed. New York, NY: Billboard Books, 2007.

Laclau, Ernesto, and Chantal Mouffe. *Hegemony and Socialist Strategy: Towards a Radical Democratic Politics*. Vol. 2nd. New York: Verso, 2001.

LaFeber, Walter. *Michael Jordan and the New Global Capitalism*. Vol. New and expanded. New York: W.W. Norton & Co., 2002.

Lee, Jooyoung. *Blowin' Up: Rap Dreams in South Central*. Chicago: University Of Chicago Press, 2016.

Leight, Elias. "The Challenge of Marketing Music on TikTok in 2024: 'The Odds of Starting Something Are So Small.'" *Billboard*, December 16, 2024. https://www.billboard.com/music/features/music-marketing-on-tiktok-not-working-2024-1235857662/.

———. "Vinyl Is Poised to Outsell CDs For the First Time Since 1986." *Rolling Stone*, September 6, 2019. https://www.rollingstone.com/music/music-news/vinyl-cds-revenue-growth-riaa-880959/.

Lesser, Bryan. "Record Labels Shot the Artists, But They Did Not Share the Equity." *The Georgetown Journal of Law & Public Policy* 16 (2018): 289–314.

Lessig, Lawrence. *Code: Version 2.0*. 2nd ed. New York: Basic Books, 2006.

Levine, Robert. "Did Drake Use AI to Say FU to Artists' Rights?" *Billboard*, April 25, 2024. https://www.billboard.com/pro/drake-ai-diss-track-artists-rights-2pac-snoop-dogg/.

Levy, Steven. "Hackers at 30: 'Hackers' and 'Information Wants to Be Free.'" *Wired*, November 21, 2014. https://www.wired.com/story/hackers-at-30-hackers-and-information-wants-to-be-free/.

Leyshon, Andrew, and Allan Watson. *The Rise of the Platform Music Industries. Digital. Newcastle upon Thyne*, UK: Agenda Publishing, 2025.

———. "User as Asset, Music as Liability: The Moral Economy of the 'Value Gap' in a Platform Musical Economy." In *The Routledge Companion to Media Industries*. Abingdon, UK: Routledge, 2021.

Litman, Jessica. *Digital Copyright*. Amherst, NY: Prometheus Books, 2006.

Malcolm, Jeremy. "Recording Industry Claims Imaginary Value Gap as a Bigger Threat Than Piracy." *Electronic Frontier Foundation*, May 17, 2017. https://www.eff.org/deeplinks/2017/05/recording-industry-claims-imaginary-value-gap-bigger-threat-piracy.

Marshall, Lee. *Bootlegging: Romanticism and Copyright in the Music Industry*. 1st ed. California: SAGE Publications Ltd, 2005.

Marx, Karl. *Capital: Volume 1: A Critique of Political Economy*. New York, NY: Penguin Classics, 1992.

———. "Economic and Philosophic Manuscripts of 1844." In The *Marx-Engels Reader*, edited by Robert C. Tucker, 2nd ed., pp. 66–125. New York: Norton, 1978.

McCarthy, Tom. "End of the Guitar? Gibson Bankruptcy Fuels Fears for Future." *The Guardian*, May 5, 2018, sec. Music. https://www.theguardian.com/music/2018/may/04/gibson-guitar-bankruptcy-ed-sheeran-martin.

McChesney, Robert Waterman. *The Problem of the Media : U.S. Communication Politics in the Twenty-First Century*. New York: Monthly Review Press, 2004.

McCourt, Tom, and Patrick Burkart. "When Creators, Corporations and Consumers Collide: Napster and the Development of On-Line Music Distribution." *Media, Culture & Society* 25, no. 3 (2003): 333–350. doi:10.1177/0163443703025003003.

McLeod, Kembrew. "Intellectual Property Law, Freedom of Expression, and the Web." In *The Politics of Information: The Electronic Mediation of Social Change*, edited by Katherine and Marc Bousquet Wills. Stanford: Alt-X Press, 2003.

Miller, Jennifer Lynn. "Diminished Citizenship: A Genealogy of the Development of 'Soft Citizenship' at the Intersection of US Mass and Political Culture." Dissertation, George Mason University, 2014. http://mars.gmu.edu/handle/1920/8857.

Mirghani, Suzannah. "The War on Piracy: Analyzing the Discursive Battles of Corporate and Government-Sponsored Anti-Piracy Media Campaigns." *Critical Studies in Media Communication* 28, no. 2 (2011): 113–134. doi:10.1080/15295036.2010.514933.

Morton, Professor David. *Off the Record: The Technology and Culture of Sound Recording in America*. New Brunswick, NJ: Rutgers University Press, 1999.

Mueller, Gavin. "Napster's Mediations." *Fast Capitalism* 21, no. 1 (2024). https://fastcapitalism.journal.library.uta.edu/index.php/fastcapitalism/article/view/501.

Negus, Keith. *Music Genres and Corporate Cultures*. New York: Routledge, 1999.

Ogg, Erica. "The Beatles Come to iTunes at Last." *CNET News*, November 16, 2010, sec. Circuit Breaker. http://news.cnet.com/8301-31021_3-20022922-260.html.

Osborne, Richard. "Masters and Slaves: Black Artists and the Ownership of Sound Recording Copyright." In *The Palgrave Handbook of Critical Music Industry Studies*, edited by David Arditi and Ryan Nolan, 33–48. New York, NY: Palgrave Macmillan, 2024. doi:10.1007/978-3-031-64013-1.

———. *Owning the Masters: A History of Sound Recording Copyright*. New York: Bloomsbury Academic, 2022.

———. "The Gold Disc: One Million Pop Fans Can't Be Wrong." In *Music by Numbers: The Use and Abuse of Statistics in the Music Industry*, edited by Richard Osborne and Dave Laing. Bristol, England: Intellect Ltd., 2021.

Palm, Michael. "Analog Backlog: Pressing Records during the Vinyl Revival." *Journal of Popular Music Studies* 29, no. 4 (2017). doi:10.1111/jpms.12247.

———. "The New Old: Vinyl Records after the Internet." In *The Dialectic of Digital Culture*, edited by David Arditi and Jennifer Miller, pp. 149–162. Lanham, MD: Lexington Books, 2019.

Pareles, Jon. "A Re-Inventor of His World and Himself – Document – Gale OneFile: Business." *The New York Times*, November 17, 1996. https://go-gale-com.ezproxy.uta.edu/ps/i.do?p=ITBC&u=txshracd2597&id=GALE%7CA150426676&v=2.1&it=r&sid=summon&aty=ip.

Park, David J. *Conglomerate Rock: The Music Industry's Quest to Divide Music and Conquer Wallets*. Lanham, MD: Lexington Books, 2007.

Patch, Justin. "Metallica, Napster and the Transformation of Subcultural Capital." *Fast Capitalism* 21, no. 1 (2024). https://fastcapitalism.journal.library.uta.edu/index.php/fastcapitalism/article/view/508.

Patel, Marilyn Hall. *A&M Records, Inc. v. Napster, Inc.*, No. C 99-5183 MHP; No. C 00-0074 MHP (United States District Court for the Northern District of California May 2000).

Patry, William. *Moral Panics and the Copyright Wars*. New York, NY: Oxford University Press, 2009.

Pham, Alex. "N.Y. Girl Settles RIAA Case." *Los Angeles Times*, September 10, 2003, sec. Music. https://www.latimes.com/archives/la-xpm-2003-sep-10-fi-girl10-story.html.

———. "The Return of Guitar Hero and Rock Band: Comeback or Throwback?" *Billboard*, July 4, 2015.

Poole, Simon. "Sorted: Categorisation and Genre in Contemporary Music Business." In *The Palgrave Handbook of Critical Music Industry Studies*, edited by David Arditi and Ryan Nolan, pp. 223–237. Cham: Springer Nature Switzerland, 2024. doi:10.1007/978-3-031-64013-1_14.

Prey, Robert. "Nothing Personal: Algorithmic Individuation on Music Streaming Platforms." *Media, Culture & Society* 40, no. 7 (2018): 1086–1100. doi:10.1177/0163443717745147.

Robertson, Adi. "'Dancing Baby' Ruling Says Fair Use Matters in Copyright Takedowns." *The Verge*, September 14, 2015. https://www.theverge.com/2015/9/14/9324549/youtube-prince-dancing-baby-copyright-fair-use-ruling.

Rolli, Bryan. "The Billboard 200 Will Incorporate YouTube Streams In 2020." *Forbes*, December 13, 2019. https://www.forbes.com/sites/bryanrolli/2019/12/13/the-billboard-200-will-incorporate-youtube-streams-in-2020/.

Saez, Catherine. "YouTube And Others Hide Behind Safe Harbours, Bigger Threat Than Piracy, Music Industry Tells WIPO." *Intellectual Property Watch*, May 4, 2017. https://www.ip-watch.org/2017/05/04/youtube-others-hide-behind-safe-harbours-bigger-threat-piracy-music-industry-says/.

Sampson, Tony D. *Virality: Contagion Theory in the Age of Networks*. 1 edition. Minneapolis: University of Minnesota Press, 2012.

Schaap, Julian, Jeroen van der Waal, and Willem de Koster. "Black Rap, White Rock: Non-Declarative Culture and the Racialization of Cultural Categories." *Sociological Inquiry* 92, no. 4 (2022): 1281–1305. doi:10.1111/soin.12461.

Scharf, Nick. "Napster's Long Shadow: Copyright and Peer-to-Peer Technology." *Journal of Intellectual Property Law & Practice* 6, no. 11 (2011): 806–812. doi:10.1093/jiplp/jpr137.

Serjeant, Jill. "Beatles Sell over 2 Million in First Week on iTunes." *Reuters*, November 24, 2010, sec. Lifestyle.

Siefert, Marsha. "Aesthetics, Technology, and the Capitalization of Culture: How the Talking Machine Became a Musical Instrument." *Science in Context* 8, no. 2 (1995): 417–449.

Sinnreich, Aram. *The Piracy Crusade: How the Music Industry's War on Sharing Destroys Markets and Erodes Civil Liberties*. Amherst: University of Massachusetts Press, 2013.

Sisario, Ben, and Michael J. de la Merced. "The Radio Giant iHeartMedia Prepares for Possible I.P.O." *The New York Times*, April 3, 2019, sec. Business. https://www.nytimes.com/2019/04/03/business/dealbook/iheartmedia-ipo-radio.html.

Skrimsjö, Veronica. "Standing in the Way of Control: The Vinyl Revival, the Record Industry, and Record Store Day." In *The Palgrave Handbook of Critical Music Industry Studies*, edited by David Arditi and Ryan Nolan, pp. 433–450. Cham: Springer Nature Switzerland, 2024. doi:10.1007/978-3-031-64013-1_26.

Slichter, Jacob. *So You Wanna Be a Rock & Roll Star: How I Machine-Gunned a Roomful of Record Executives and Other True Tales from a Drummer's Life*. New York: Broadway Books, 2004.

Smith, Adam. *An Inquiry into the Nature and Causes of the Wealth of Nations*. Digireads.com, 2009.

Smith, Paul. "Tommy Hilfiger in the Age of Mass Customization." In *No Sweat: Fashion, Free Trade, and the Rights of Garment Workers*, edited by Andrew Ross. London: Verso, 1997.

Smythe, Dallas Walker. "On the Audience Commodity and Its Work." In *Dependency Road: Communications, Capitalism, Consciousness, and Canada*, edited by Dallas Walker Smythe, pp. 230–256. Norwood, NJ: Ablex, 1981.

SoundScan 1996 Year-End Music Industry Report. *Nielsen*, January 7, 1997.

SoundScan 1998 Year-End Music Industry Report. *Nielsen*, January 6, 1999.

SoundScan 2000 Year-End Music Industry Report. *Nielsen*, January 3, 2001.

SoundScan 2002 Year-End Music Industry Report. *Nielsen*, January 2, 2003.
SoundScan 2004 Year-End Music Industry Report. *Nielsen*, January 5, 2005.
SoundScan 2006 Year-End Music Industry Report. *Nielsen*, January 4, 2007.
SoundScan 2010 Year-End Music Industry Report. *Nielsen*, January 5, 2011.
Sousa, John Philip. "Letter to the Editor of the 'Daily Mail.'" In *Through the Year with Sousa: Excerpts from the Operas, Marches, Miscellaneous Compositions, Novels, Letters, Magazine Articles, Songs, Sayings and Rhymes of John Philip Sousa*, pp. 145–146. New York, NY T. Y. Crowell & Company, 1910.
———. "The Menace of Mechanical Music." *Appleton's Magazine*, 1906. https://explorepahistory.com/odocument.php?docId=1-4-1A1.
Staff. "Billboard 200 to Include Official Video Plays From YouTube, Streaming Services." *Billboard*, December 13, 2019. https://www.billboard.com/pro/billboard-200-changes-youtube-video-data-streaming-album-charts/.
———. "Billboard Finalizes Changes to How Streams Are Weighted for Billboard Hot 100 & Billboard 200." *Billboard*, May 1, 2018. https://www.billboard.com/pro/billboard-changes-streaming-weighting-hot-100-billboard-200/.
Sterne, Jonathan. MP3: *The Meaning of a Format*. Durham, NC: Duke University Press, 2012.
Szrot, Lukas. "Independent Music after Metallica v. Napster, Inc.: Seeking Liberation in the Music Streaming Simulacrum." *Fast Capitalism* 21, no. 1 (2024). https://fastcapitalism.journal.library.uta.edu/index.php/fastcapitalism/article/view/506.
Szu Yu Chen. "Pop Songs Are Getting Shorter in the Era of Streaming and TikTok." *Washington Post*. May 18, 2025. https://www.washingtonpost.com/entertainment/interactive/2024/shorter-songs-again/.
Taylor, P.C. "Funky White Boys and Honorary Soul Sisters." *Michigan Quarterly Review* 36, no. 2 (1997): 320–335.
Thanawala, Sudhin. "YouTube Video of Baby Dancing to Prince Track Sparks Trial over Copyright." *CBC News*, September 15, 2015. https://www.cbc.ca/news/entertainment/youtube-video-of-baby-dancing-to-prince-track-sparks-trial-over-copyright-1.3228580.
Tolstad, Ingrid M. "'The Numbers Don't Lie!': Metrics as Tools for Decision Making and Strategic Planning in Music Industry Organizations." In *The Palgrave Handbook of Critical Music Industry Studies*, edited by David Arditi and Ryan Nolan, pp. 209–221. Cham: Springer Nature Switzerland, 2024. doi:10.1007/978-3-031-64013-1_13.
Vaidhyanathan, Siva. *Copyrights and Copywrongs: The Rise of Intellectual Property and How It Threatens Creativity*. New York: NYU Press, 2003.
Wang, Amy X. "Guitars Aren't Dying. They're as Popular as Ever." *Rolling Stone*, May 22, 2018. https://www.rollingstone.com/pro/news/guitars-are-getting-more-popular-so-why-do-we-think-theyre-dying-630446/.
———. "Music's New Chart Rules Care – a Lot – About Whether You're Paying to Listen." *Rolling Stone*, May 3, 2018. https://www.rollingstone.com/pro/news/musics-new-chart-rules-care-a-lot-about-whether-youre-paying-to-listen-628957/.
Watkins, S. Craig. *Don't Knock the Hustle: Young Creatives, Tech Ingenuity, and the Making of a New Innovation Economy*. Beacon Press, 2019.
———. *Hip Hop Matters: Politics, Pop Culture, and the Struggle for the Soul of a Movement*. Boston: Beacon Press, 2005.

Watson, Allan, and Andrew Leyshon. "Negotiating Platformisation: MusicTech, Intellectual Property Rights and Third Wave Platform Reintermediation in the Music Industry." *Journal of Cultural Economy* 15, no. 3 (2022): 326–343. doi:10.1080/17530350.2022.2028653.

Watson, Allan, Joseph B. Watson, and Lou Tompkins. "Does Social Media Pay for Music Artists? Quantitative Evidence on the Co-Evolution of Social Media, Streaming and Live Music." *Journal of Cultural Economy* 16, no. 1 (2023): 32–46. doi:10.1080/17530350.2022.2087720.

Yankovic, *"Weird Al." Don't Download This Song. Straight Outta Lynwood.* Los Angeles, CA: Volcano, 2006.

INDEX

360 deal 33

A&M Records, Inc. v Napster, Inc. 26, 29
access 47
Adorno, Theodor 4, 17, 43, 58–59
ad-supported 11, 44, 46–48, 53
advance 11, 13, 22, 33, 62
affordance 14, 55, 59
Aglietta, Michel 17
album replacement cycle 10, 15–16, 18–20, 23, 25–26, 35–36
  CD replacement cycle 16
algorithmic exploitation (AE) 61–63
alienation 1
Anderton, Chris 1, 41–42
Apple Music 29, 40, 42, 44–46, 49, 60
artificial intelligence (AI) 3, 11, 30, 56, 62–63

Bandcamp 44, 49
The Beatles 36
Beats Music 29, 49
Before the Music Dies 56
Ben-Yehuda, Nachman 5–6
Betamax case 10, 14
BigChampagne 43
Billboard 43–44, 46, 48, 50, 53–54, 56, 60
  Billboard 200, 46, 53–54
  Billboard Magazine 43–44, 46, 48, 50, 53–54, 56, 60
  Hot 100 46, 53, 60
bit-torrents 11, 29, 40
British Phonographic Industry (BPI) 10, 13, 22, 56

Californian ideology 28
capital 3, 14, 22, 28, 34, 49, 51
capitalism 1–2, 17, 22, 29, 36, 42, 48, 52, 58

capitalist 17, 30, 54–55, 58
cassette 10, 13–15, 18–23, 25, 31, 36, 43, 49, 59
catalog 16–17, 19–20, 23, 28, 36, 47
celestial jukebox 28, 40, 45, 47
ChatGPT 63
Cohen, Stanley 4
commodity 2–3, 35, 55–56, 59
compact disc (CD) 5, 10, 14, 16–17, 19–22, 26–29, 31–37, 40–43, 48–49, 57, 59
  CD-R 10, 19, 22, 26, 35–36
  CD-ROM 19, 36
  CD-RW 10, 19, 22, 35
competition 2, 7, 15, 26, 31, 35–36
consumption 3–4, 17–19, 28, 38, 42–43, 46, 50, 54–56, 63
  defined 42
  democratic 43, 50, 54–55
copyright 3–4, 6–8, 25, 28–29, 33–34, 39, 42, 48, 50, 61–62
  performance rights 33, 42
  publishing rights 33
  sound recording 16, 32–33, 40, 42, 57
culture 1, 3, 6, 8–10, 13–14, 17, 21–23, 29–30, 36, 40–41, 43, 46, 49, 54, 56–60, 64
  defined 21

dead music 64
democratic consumption 43, 50, 54–55
Digital Millennium Copyright Act (DMCA) 45
Digital Performance Right in Sound Recordings Act (DPRA) 42, 46
Dr. Dre 29, 49
Drake 63

Electronic Frontier Foundation (EFF) 39, 50

fair use 14, 39
Fairness in Music Licensing Act of 1998 20
fear 4, 6, 9–10, 21, 62
fidelity 15–16, 18–20, 57
file-sharing 3–6, 11, 25–32, 34, 37, 40, 43, 45, 49, 57, 62
   peer-2-peer (p2p) 27–29
folk devil 3–4, 8, 11, 13, 40, 50, 53, 56, 60–61
freemium 47, 49, 53

Goode, Erich Goode 5–6
Grammys 51–52, 56, 59
gramophone 1, 15, 17, 55, 59, 61
Grand Theft Auto 37
Guitar Hero 37

hegemony 21–22
Hollywood 9, 14, 40
home taping 4, 10, 13–15, 19, 21–23
Horkheimer, Max 4, 17, 43, 58

ideology 5, 22, 28, 51
independent
   artists 14, 15, 21–22, 27–28, 30–31, 48
   music 3, 15, 21–23, 26–28, 35, 48–49
indie 3
Instagram 60
International Federation of the Phonographic Industry (IFPI) 11, 16, 18–19, 25–26, 29–30, 32, 35–37, 40, 48, 50–53, 56
iTunes Store 5, 11, 26, 28–30, 34, 36, 45, 49

just-in-time production 35

Leyshon, Andrew 44–45, 53, 61–62
lifestyle music 37
live music 1–2, 41

Marx, Karl 2, 51
master recording 16, 32–33, 40
   remaster 16
means of consumption 17–18
means of production 2, 13, 21, 62
Metallica 4, 11, 28–29, 34
Moore, Frances 50

mp3 25, 27, 34, 36, 57, 59
music genome 44, 58
Music panic 8, 11
music streaming platforms (MSPs) 40–41, 43, 45–49, 51–54, 58–60, 62

Napster 3, 5, 11, 25–31, 34–35, 40, 49, 57
NBA YoungBoy 46
Nielsen 35, 46
   SoundScan 35, 46, 48, 53–54

Pandora Radio 42, 44, 47, 58
panic narrative 3–6, 8, 10–11, 13, 15, 22, 25–26, 31–32, 36–37, 40, 53–54, 56, 63
   music 10, 63
   piracy 3, 5–6, 11, 13, 15, 22, 25–26, 31, 36–37, 40, 53
piracy 3–8, 11, 13–16, 19–20, 22–23, 25–26, 30–32, 34, 36–37, 40, 50, 52–53, 56
planned obsolescence 15, 18
platform 11, 27–30, 40, 43–47, 49–50, 52–53, 58, 61–62
Portnow, Neil 51, 56
Prince 39–40, 45
profit 2, 11, 22, 29, 47, 51, 55–56, 63–64
pro-rata 41

radio 10, 13–14, 21, 27, 40, 42–44, 56, 58
   internet 42, 44
   satellite 42
   terrestrial 42, 44
record contract 2, 32–33, 39–40, 52, 60, 62
   360 deal 33
record labels 2, 3–4, 10–11, 13–23, 25–29, 31–32, 34, 36–37, 40, 42–49, 51–53, 55–56, 58, 60–63
recorded music 1–3, 5, 9, 14–16, 22, 33, 53, 55, 64
Recording Academy (National Academy of Recording Arts & Sciences) 51
   Grammy Creators Alliance 52
   Grammys 51, 56
Recording Industry Association of America (RIAA) 11, 15, 20, 25–26, 28–29, 31–35, 37, 40, 56, 63

Recording Industry in Numbers (RIN) 16, 18–19, 29–30, 32, 35–37, 53
recoup 22, 33
Red Hot Chili Peppers 27, 31
renumeration 11, 41, 48
Rock Band 37
Rosen, Hilary 31
royalties 7, 14, 20, 33, 42, 46

shipment 16–17, 35
social media 3, 60–62
Sony Music Entertainment (*also* Sony) 10, 14, 18, 47, 63
SoundCloud 44, 49–50
Sousa, John Philip 6–9, 61
Spears, Britney 32
Spotify 3, 40, 42–49, 52–53, 59
streaming 11, 20, 29, 40–41, 43, 45, 47–51, 53–54, 56–57, 59, 62
  culture 29, 41
  defined 41
  subscriber 29, 48–49

subscription 11, 20, 28–29, 41, 45, 47–49, 53
surplus value 2, 51

Telecommunications Act of 1996 44
TikTok 59–61
Timbaland 63

unauthorized reproduction 7–8, 11, 63
unending consumption 28
Universal Music Group (*also* Universal) 10, 14, 39–40, 47, 63

value gap 11, 50–52, 56, 62
Victrola 1
video games 37
vinyl 10, 13, 16, 18–19, 21, 29, 49, 57, 59
  LP 16–17, 20, 23, 36, 59
viral 60–61

Warner Music Group 47, 63
Watson, Alan 44–45, 53, 61–62

Yankovic, Weird Al 25–26, 31–32
YouTube 39–40, 43–46, 50, 52–54, 60–61

www.ingramcontent.com/pod-product-compliance
Lightning Source LLC
Chambersburg PA
CBHW030143170426
43199CB00008B/185